Love to Live by

Praise for Love to Live By

This is an inspirational collection of vignettes that are true depictions of "living love." This book is filled with anecdotes to achieve true happiness and deep spirituality... A remarkable read for those who need true inspiration to triumph over adversities and the everyday stress of life.

—Marcelle S. Balcombe, Esq.
Sichenzia Ross Ference Kesner LLP

There is no doubt that the wisdom contained in this book will open your mind, expand your heart, and change your life. From cinnamon rolls to eternal life, with everything in between, her observations are thought provoking and revealing. Buy it, read it, and let Karen inspire you as she has inspired so many the world over."

—Anita Debney, Entrepreneur/Consultant

I feel so grateful to have Karen Nelson's wisdom at my fingertips. I have known her for many years as a dear friend. During our friendship we conceived children who met, fell in love, and married each other. We now share our grandchildren. I deeply know Karen to be true to her words in her book. She lives love and my grandchildren and I have been greatly blessed and will continue to be blessed by her love eternally.

—Leslie Brown, LMHC EMDR,
Consultant/Facilitator/Trainer

What a rare opportunity to see into the mind and read the thoughts of an extraordinary woman who not only radiates love, but has become love to everyone in her circle of influence... Reading this book could be a life changer.

—Rojean Garnica,
Literary Teacher/Writer

Love to Live by

Things I Would Want My Children to Know

Karen Mann Nelson

Larksong Publishing
SANTA BARBARA

Chapter epigraphs: Karen Mann Nelson
Cover design: Kimberley Hirt
Cover painting: Josie Summerhays
Editing & interior design: Tanya Brockett, www.HallagenInk.com

Unless otherwise noted, scriptural references are from the King James Version of *The Bible* at www.BibleGateway.com, and *The Book of Mormon* and *Doctrine and Covenants* from The Church of Jesus Christ of Latter-Day Saints via www.LDS.org/scriptures.

I write these words to thank God for the life He has allowed me the chance to adventure through, bask in, and "stand all amazed at."

I dedicate these writings to Honor and Privilege. It has been mine. Seeing love through God's eyes is all my life.

LOVE
is always the way
always the answer
always the healer
the voice
the magic
the wonder
the dance
the miracle
the ocean
the light
the laugh
the always
TO LIVE BY

—KAREN MANN NELSON

Contents

Foreword	 xiii
Preface	 xv
Chapter One	Inspired Living 1
Chapter Two	Loving One Another 17
Chapter Three	Be Happy 29
Chapter Four	Love & Marriage 41
Chapter Five	Parenting & Children 53
Chapter Six	Friends 75
Chapter Seven	A Mother's Love 85
Chapter Eight	Family Relationships 105
Chapter Nine	Abiding in Faith 123
Chapter Ten	Giving & Being of Service 135
Chapter Eleven	Talents & Gifts 145

Chapter Twelve   Living Happily & Well 177

Chapter Thirteen   Keeping the Faith 195

Chapter Fourteen   Words to Live By 207

Chapter Fifteen   Thoughts to Ponder 219

Afterword   Things I Would Want My
                        Children to Know.................... 231

About the Author   235

Foreword

Seldom in this lifetime do you meet someone and feel an immediate connection. If you are ever fortunate enough to have this experience, grab hold and allow the relationship to grow. Nurture it with words and thoughts and deeds, for it is a gift from God that must be treasured for eternity.

What I am describing is exactly what I experienced when I first met Karen. She was teaching a lesson at church and she shared a story about one of her children. In an instant, I was taken back to my own childhood and feeling my mother's love for me. Tears flowed down my cheeks as I recalled the personal struggle my mother had been going through on that day. It had been fifty years and it was as if no time had passed at all.

After the lesson, I went up to the front of the room to introduce myself and to thank her for sharing her message. I can even remember the dress she wore that day; it was olive green and covered with larger than life flowers. Yet I did not tell her about the profound effect her words had had upon me that day. Why didn't I say anything? Because I wanted to get to know Karen and experience more of her gentle magic firsthand.

That was three years ago and these days I consider Karen to be my most special friend in this world. She has a timeless quality that enables me to time travel at will. She has a wisdom that brings me closer to philosophers and sages. And she is a relentless warrior when it comes to protecting and serving her family members and close friends. Yes, Karen is a unique and special gift from the Lord to me and to those whose lives she touches.

Read this book as though she is speaking to you. Imagine that the love she is expressing for her family is actually meant for you. Truly hear her stories and experiences as if they were your own. Visualize her sitting next to you, taking your hands in hers, and telling you what you already know but may have long since forgotten. For in reading what Karen has written here, we are all so much closer to experiencing God's love for each of us.

—*Connie Ragen Green*

Preface

I woke up today to my husband heading out the door to play tennis. I looked in on our sleepyhead sixteen year old and an accumulation of friends that kept showing up after we had gone to bed. There were signs of guitar playing, towels were draped everywhere from jacuzzi play, fruit roll-up wrappers were strewn here and there, and sunshine gleamed through the hundreds of palm trees surrounding our home.

I then prayed a prayer of deep gratitude, and earnest, faithful yearning for those I love. My prayers are long, thankfully, because of the gift of ten magnificent children, six fabulous son- and daughter-in-laws, who are really our children, and twelve fun, fascinating grandchildren.

Then I sat down to write, which is my most favorite thing in the whole world, along with walking and biking on the beach, yoga, sewing, singing, sitting around the table with my family doing anything, painting, and laundry. These things I love are a clearing and watering of the mind for me. What I am getting at is, I get to do what I love.

Above all else, way above all else, are the people in my life. I love my people, all of them, everyone I have ever known, and each of those particular souls assigned to me, that I will have to get to heaven to find words to express gratitude for.

Then, I danced to Michael Jackson, one of my "passion for his art" luminaries, walked around my yard breathing in God's ocean air, picked and ate a plum and tangerine off our trees, and then came back to write. We have raised our children all over the world, but somehow the core of my loves have always stayed the same.

At BYU, we raised our new angel on campus with alternating schedules until we graduated. In Washington DC, we balanced our both working at the Capitol with our angel firstborn. In Concord, we raised little ones by a lake. In Belmont, I put our babies in an English pram, and headed out every day to see what we could see in our little town. In Chelmsford, we threw in lots of snow play and ice-skating. In England, we lived much of our life on the Tube to discover our new land and surrounding countries. In Fremont our life was a tangerine tree and brown babies that were never out of the pool. Bothell, Washington, was the pinnacle—two and a half acres of wonderland forest with all our children finally all born and there! Bunnies, baby bunnies, cats, and kitties, Indiana (the greatest dog in the universe), endless puppies, a spiral staircase, and a dinosaur tree in a forest glen were our perfect.

Highland, Utah, was next and it was our greatest mixture of everything happening all at once. Elementary, junior high, high school, and college kids and their friends, and sometimes forty people for Sunday Dinner was our happiness. Then back to Santa Barbara where I mostly grew up, along with being raised in Washington, DC, four times, Arizona, San Francisco, and Venezuela.

I have kept journals throughout my life. I occasionally open them up randomly. Sometimes there is bliss, sometimes there is heartache, sometimes there is joy that makes me cry for an hour, sometimes there is sadness that makes me cry for hours, sometimes it looks like a horror show of chaos, and sometimes it looks like joy beyond anything I could have ever dreamed of or imagined, ever.

The combination of these kinds of living love have brightened, deepened, and expanded my everything. I know for sure that I am grateful for it all. In the beginning, I would probably have used watercolors to paint my life. In the middle of it all, I would have used dark, rich, brilliant oil paint. Now, I think I would paint with acrylics, a medium that allows for the freedom and lightness of water-base with the richness of weight. My painting is the most beautiful thing I have ever seen, because it is mine. It took everything I ever had or am or went through to paint it. My words are my hope for bringing each brush stroke to you, my loved ones.

*Catching the message is
how you catch the moments.*

CHAPTER ONE

Inspired Living

BEING "FOR" PEOPLE

We should be one another's cheerleader as we watch each other pursue our own unique talents—be encouraging, always urging forward, and inspiring.

Whenever there is a need for help in the form of encouragement or prayer, my children start texting long strings of messages back and forth between them, whether it is for a test, or college entrance, or a spiritual, emotional, or physical concern. I love reading this outpouring of love between them, and I know the energy and power of their faith and love is real, sustaining, and healing.

INVISIBILITY

This is a concept that enables you to be so in tune with the Lord's will that you become dissolved in His work. It is at this point that you "disappear" and become a perfect vessel or conduit through which the Lord can work—whether it be in speech or action.

And then, accompanied with what is uniquely within you—deeply embedded into the very core of who you are—a rich, pure gift is able to be given, hand in hand with God.

NO ONE MISSING

We should do everything in our power to help each other along life's journey so when we sit down in heaven together, there will be "no one missing." My sister-in-law and I woke up with the same dream one morning. Our families were sitting on a white bench in heaven, and everyone was laughing. In the dream, no one was missing.

NOBILITY

My friend and I were at a garage sale where a huge sign had been posted, "All Prices Negotiable." She found a small, framed print that was priced at $2.00, so she offered $1.00. The woman in charge of the garage sale looked up at my friend and then called out to all the other women in the garage and announced, haughtily, "Can you believe the nerve of some people. This was obviously priced so far below what it was worth. I can't believe this!"

Everyone immediately became very quiet at the awkwardness of the situation.

My friend simply approached the woman and said quietly, "I'm sorry." She then placed the picture down on the table and left.

Noble acts not only reveal a lack thereof in others, but after reflection, also inspire them to seek nobility for themselves.

IF YOU DON'T HAVE IT

If you don't have it, you don't want it badly enough. That is how you can really tell how much you care about something: you either have it or you are avidly pursuing it.

"I wish I could play the piano; I wish I were an Olympian; I wish I could travel the world; I wish I could have a motorcycle; I wish I could get a PhD; I wish I could write a book; I wish I could sing and dance; or I wish I was an artist."

If you are what you want or you have what you want then you must have wanted it badly enough.

Candles

In the story, *Les Miserables*, a priest gives a vagabond a pair of silver candlesticks that the vagabond had just stolen from him. The man was about to be arrested, but was instead released with the candlesticks and a plea from the priest to use the money from the sale of the candlesticks to seek a better life, which he did. If we could purchase a "whole soul" with one kind deed...

Remember Him

Remembering Him will change everything you do in life. It has huge power to direct your every thought and choice. He is willing to be the master and guide for your soul, if you choose to let Him lead you.

Let it Flow

I believe when we wake up in the morning and pray to ask the Lord to guide us through the day, we can count on just that. It is simple faith to believe, absolutely, that He will. I do not think we have to overwork the process that may move us into a lack of faith. I believe we can trust Him and let it flow. Let the spirit flow through us as we flow through our day. He is there.

CHOOSE POORLY

It is the God-given right of every human soul to choose poorly and make bad decisions. When my children speak of the injustices that cause them hurt or pain, I say to them, "I am sorry that they chose poorly."

We only have control over our own lives and we must respect the right of others to choose as they will. It is God's way.

TURN OFF THE MUSIC

Sometimes it is better to turn off the music, even if it is Mozart. I never want to play the radio in the car because I want to think. Or if someone is with me, I want to hear what he or she is saying.

There is just too much music—iPods in ears, music playing constantly in the home—turning it off allows you to hear bird voices, the wind, and most importantly, the sounds of your loved ones speaking. Imagine how wasted a walk along the beach would be with iPod earphones in your ears. A lot of "real life" is wasted this way.

OCEAN

Go to the ocean whenever you possibly can. You will see why.

YOU GET TO KEEP IT

Loved ones pass away. We leave homes we dearly love. Beloved pets grow old and leave us. Children grow up and move away. Everything keeps leaving and passing, but we get to keep it all. It is in our hearts forever: memorized, remembered, and held sacred.

Life is not about losing; it is about gaining. My daughter taught me this when she quoted Dr. Seuss to me one day, "Don't cry because it is over; smile because it happened."

IT LIVES

"My father says almost the whole world is asleep...everybody you know, everybody you see, everybody you talk to. He says only a few people are awake, and they live in a state of constant total amazement."

—From the movie, *Joe Versus the Volcano*

"Every man dies, not every man lives."

—From the movie, *Braveheart*

"Life moves pretty fast. If you don't stop and look around once in a while, you might miss it."

—From the movie, *Ferris Bueller's Day Off*

"Don't ask what the world needs. Ask what makes you come alive, and go and do it. Because what the world needs are people who have come alive."

—Howard Thurman, Author/Philosopher

"The desire to create is one of the deepest yearnings of the human soul. No matter our talents, education, backgrounds, or abilities, we each have an inherent wish to create something."

—Dieter F. Uchtdorf, Aviator/Airline
Executive/Religious Leader

"Whatever Jesus lays his hands upon, lives. If He lays his hands upon a marriage, it lives. If He is allowed to lay His hands upon a family, it lives."

—Howard W. Hunter, Lawyer/
LDS Church President

My father says, "The only truly 'wealthy' person is someone who is able to spend their lives doing something they truly love."

My brother-in-law has flown fighter planes for the air force his entire career. He says that he is always amazed when he gets paid for doing this because he loves it so much.

At age thirty-four, my daughter just discovered what she really wants to do in life, and she says it is the first time she has felt "alive" for very long time.

We owe it to ourselves, the world, and to God to wake up and find out what makes us come alive and then "live" it. God can help us discover what that is because He knows—He created us.

HOLY

And members shall manifest before the church, by a godly walk and conversation, walking in holiness before the Lord. (DC 20:60)

But as he which hath called you is holy, so be ye holy in all manner of conversation. (1 Peter 1:15 KJV)

For thou art an holy people unto the Lord thy God: the Lord thy God hath chosen thee to be a special people unto himself, above all people that are upon the face of the earth. (Deuteronomy 7:6 KJV)

The spirit of the lord doth not dwell in unholy temples. (Helaman 4:24)

Be ye holy; for I am holy. (1 Peter 1:16 KJV)

Taking the word "holy" into my heart as I go forward each day seems to make a difference in the choices I make: in what I watch, how I speak, how I spend money, how I think, the clothes I wear, how I spend my time and energy, and what I listen to. One word.

SHARP

We all make sure we run back from the car to return the pen we accidentally kept. Words, however, present a different challenge. To keep honesty "sharp," I make sure I am very specific about how I represent something. I will say "ten days" instead of "two weeks" or "it was around $30.00" instead of "about $20.00," if the price was $28.99 (for instance).

Most people won't notice or care about the small corrections you make in your attempt to be completely honest, but these private victories strengthen your determination to be honest in word and deed.

"WHY ARE YOU DOING THAT?"

My daughter was watching me do yoga stretches and noticed I was doing them in a more exaggerated way than what was being shown on the video. She asked me why and I said, "So it is harder."

Whether you casually exercise or not, it is still the same one hour you are investing, so try to get the most out of it.

OVERTHINKING

Too much information on *every single thing* in the universe is causing an epidemic of people who are overthinking "living."

Those who overthink what they eat are often the least healthy people. Those who overthink and over "do" working out are often the people in need of regular recovery from illness and injury. When faced with a decision to make, we often let Google decide what is right for us, instead of gathering all the facts (which is the great part of our age of information) and then listening to our minds, hearts, and the voice within us. Our minds and bodies will actually "talk" to us if we let them. We can then make "living life" choices that are clear-minded, physically healthy, and spiritually guided.

SELF-DESTRUCTION CYCLE

If someone does not feel that he is worthy to be successful, beautiful, wealthy, healthy, happy, etc., he will enter a self-destruction cycle that will never end until he looks up to God and asks, "What do you think of me?" God is the only one we should base the ultimate source of our self-esteem upon. God truly knows us and deeply cares about us. He will tell us who we are and how worthy we are of sustainable happiness.

MOM'S HEALTHY HINTS

- Ask yourself, "Is this food, or whatever it is I am doing, my friend or my enemy?"
- Drink several glasses of water when you first wake up before eating any food, and wait at least fifteen minutes before you eat. Drink a huge glass of water before going to bed, and if you happen to wake up in the night, drink more water. Turn your body into a "washing machine" to keep yourself healthy.
- Drink a huge glass of water fifteen to thirty minutes before eating a big meal. Never drink any liquid during a meal. You can begin drinking water again an hour after you eat. This allows your body to digest your food in the most efficient way without diluting the effort.
- Soda pop is poison.
- Exercise a minimum of three times per week. It doesn't matter what you do, although you

will find yourself able to do it better and more often if it is an exercise you enjoy. You can exercise five or six times per week if you want.

- Grandma Bessie's exercise motto: "Every day until the day you die!"
- Always eat breakfast—never skip.
- Yoga is good to do anytime, but it especially keeps you flexible as you age. It is also great during pregnancy.
- Early to bed, early to rise: good sleep helps with good health, weight loss, and stress reduction, while it increases mental awareness and creativity!
- Whatever you have decided to do to increase health, start now instead of tomorrow, or Monday, or next week, or after the holidays.
- Processed foods and white bread are like eating pure sugar.
- Use your own mind and body to teach you what you need to eat.
- Celebrate life with the foods you choose and how you live your life. In the scriptures it says that the purpose of food is to "enliven the soul."

PERSONAL

In the movie, *You've Got Mail*, the new mega bookstore in town is stealing away all the business that had been going to the little town bookstore. After Kathleen Kelly's store closes, the owner of the mega store, Joe Fox, says, "It wasn't personal."

She replies, "What's that supposed to mean? I am so sick of that. All that means is that it wasn't personal to you. But it was personal to me. It's 'personal' to a lot of people. And what's so wrong with being personal, anyway?"

Joe Fox then replies, "Uh, nothing."

To which she replies, "Whatever else anything is, it ought to begin by being personal."

I believe every single, "It wasn't personal," is accompanied by very personal, deeply felt, hurt feelings of someone we love and would never want to hurt by our "un-personal" acts or words. Let's be personal!

WORTH A QUESTION

Everything is worth a question. The answer will always be "No!" until you ask. In our family, everyone's life has been greatly altered and blessed by living this way. The secret is to always ask the one at the top (i.e., president) because he cares about your experience with their college, or hospital, or car dealership, or fast food store, etc.

I think we also do not ask God enough. Nephi, in the Book of Mormon declares, "Yea, I know that God will give liberally to him that asketh" (2 Nephi 4:35). He is standing open armed, waiting to bless us with "all that He hath." I think we forget to ask for all the miracles and blessings He is anxious to pour out upon us. Our faith combined with His hope that we will "look to God and live" is powerful beyond our imagining. He is the "president" of the world and He most definitely cares about our lives.

LIKE HENRY

Henry, who was three years old at the time, was asked what it was like to go to Lego Land. He looked up and said, "It was an awesome good time, and I was awesome!"

Everyone should feel about himself or herself the way Henry feels about himself. When he walks in a room, he throws up his arms and jumps and smiles and laughs and spins in circles and stoops down and then springs up in the air and dances. It is like he is announcing with his body, "Here I am, I am Henry, and I am the happy to be me and to be alive and I am amazing and cool and awesome, and so are you, so let's live and love life together."

One time he was hiding behind a towel and I told him to show me his beautiful face. He pulled the towel away and said, "I have the most beautiful face in the whole world. Jesus is good." He then proceeded to sing a song about Jesus as he ran out of the room. I believe Jesus would love it if we could remember what Henry knows—that we are awesome and beautiful.

Anyhow, anywhere, anytime are all dwarfed
by the power of anyway.

CHAPTER TWO

Loving One Another

HOLD BACK

In the movie *Always*, there is a line that says, "The love we hold back is the only pain that follows us here." When we choose not to love, we lose and regret. When we choose to love, we gain and find joy.

MILLSTONE CRIMES

In the scriptures, it talks about how it would be better for someone who offends a little one to have been drowned in the ocean with a millstone tied around his neck. This is a powerful image used to describe the greatness of this offense.

WITHOUT COMPLETE UNDERSTANDING

In the movie *A River Runs Through It*, there is a line that says, "So it is those we live with and should know who elude us. But we can still love them—we can love completely without complete understanding." Perfect living is not a requirement for perfect loving.

AFTER ALL THIS

I have thought about all the things we go through in a lifetime—so many trials, joys, experiences, and adventures—and I think, "after all this, and then not win?"

I want to live in heaven with all the people I love. We need to help each other through it all so we can all "win" together—so we can win eternal life together.

BE ON THEIR SIDE

If you find yourself in a contentious situation, stop and take a moment to jump over to their side. We should be fighting *for* each other, not against each other. Our goal is to be one in love and harmony.

Get on their side and stay on their side. If you fight for them, you fight for yourself as well.

Don't Take it Personally

When my children come to me in distress and look right into my eyes with the most troubled of expressions and passionate exclamations, I think to myself, *don't take it personally*. All appearances lead you to believe they are angry with you, but they never are. They are upset about something that is happening in their lives that is greatly upsetting them. In those situations, letting the phrase "don't take it personally" run through my mind has allowed me to "absorb" their distress and respond compassionately instead of reactively.

There is a perfect example in the *Book of Mormon* in Alma 61:9. Pahoran writes to Moroni, "In your epistle you have censured me, but it mattereth not; I am not angry, but rejoice in the greatness of your heart." He closes his epistle, "my beloved, brother Moroni."

Imagine the effect it would have on a loved one if after having been censured we said, "It mattereth not; I am not angry, but rejoice in the greatness of your heart." We could follow that by seeking to discover exactly what it is in "their life" that is causing them to be upset.

Moroni had great cause for being upset with what was happening in his life. The Lamanites were coming upon them, taking their lands, and murdering their people. He was most certainly upset with what was happening in his life. Pahoran knew it and responded with love, concern, and the needed counsel and help.

YELLING AT GOD

When children yell at you in anguish, you absorb their pain, and love them through their sorrows.

That is what God does. He doesn't mind if we "yell" at Him. He wants to hear our cries, He wants us to turn to Him at "all" times: happy, sad, grateful, angry, miserable, and rejoicing. He loves, loves, loves us, just like we love, love, love our children. He doesn't mind at all if we yell. He is there to absorb it all—just as we are there to absorb it all for our children.

Our children turn to us, and our loving responses teach them that they can trust God as we have learned to trust Him and His infinite love for us.

TOUCH

The other day, I went into my son's room because he said he wanted to talk to me about something. I went in and sat on his bed. He then said, "No, I changed my mind. I don't want to talk about it anymore."

Without even thinking, I put my hand on his shoulder and just sat there for a second. Then he started talking about what was troubling him. I realized, later, that it was because I touched his shoulder that he felt open and safe. Touch is also a spiritual connection.

GO FOR THE GOLD

Jesus Christ sacrificed His life at the request of our Heavenly Father by partaking of the bitter cup and treading the wine press alone. From all that was involved in the sacrifice—the "great" drops of blood shed (also great because He was great), the words of forgiveness that showered over the world from the cross, and the culminating victory at the tomb—the power to heal sprang from the power of the love in the sacrifice.

I have found that this love, introduced into the world by Jesus Christ, can take the blackest black and turn it into the whitest white. But then something spectacularly wonderful, even "magical," happens—it all turns gold in the end. It turns from black to white to gold. If we let Him heal us, and keep our minds firm and holding on to the healing, we will live our lives in the gold. If we do not go back to the black by weakness of will or mind, a gold purer than any found on earth will be ours because it was paid for at a high and heavy cost—the blood of the Lamb of God. There is a song with the words: consider the lilies of the field...how they grow; consider the birds of the sky...how they fly; consider the sheep of His fold...He knows the meadows where they feed...and He will heal those who trust Him and make their hearts as gold.

KISS MORE

I read some scientific research about kissing that said this connection is powerful on so many more levels than we might think, and it keeps people tied to each other. Kiss all your loved ones all the time and watch the love connections grow.

MAD

If someone's words or behavior disappoints or frustrates you, make their bed or clean their closet or make them food or give them a gift or do anything else you can think of to "serve" them. Doing so grows love back faster than anything I have ever found. Pray over them also. Somehow in the process, you remember how blessed you are to have them in your life.

ASSUME
Assume people love you. To know someone is to love them, so just assume that they either love you now or they will as soon as they get to know you.

EYES
Make people look at you. Do not let them avert their eyes while they talk to you. Hold their face in your hands (if you are comfortable doing that). Do whatever it takes; they need to know and feel that you love them. It will go into them through their eyes.

"WHAT'S NOT TO LIKE"
In the movie Enchanted, someone asks the prince if he likes himself. He is sitting on a bed, looks left and right, and says, "What's not to like?"

We should feel like that about ourselves and everyone else around us.

STROKING HAIR
At night when I tuck in my children, I sing them "their" lullaby and stoke their hair while I sing the

song. Over the years, I have noticed that whenever I was sad or sick, my youngest child would stay by me and stroke my hair until I felt better. I think if God were actually present in those situations, He might do that exact thing.

No Defense Against Love

Since there is no defense against the greatest power on earth, if you keep at it, you will win. If you have offended someone beyond imaginable repair, begin imagining. It may even take years, but you will break them down with the determined, unwavering demonstrations of your love. The power is too great—the human spirit will succumb.

Ice Crystals: "Two Nice Things"

"Don't say that, you are damaging your ice crystals! Okay, now you have to say two nice things about that person (or yourself)."

This is commonly heard in our home when someone says something negative about themselves or someone else.

Japanese scientist Masaru Emoto (2005) researched the effect that words have on the freezing process of water. Words were spoken and music was played as water froze and the difference was astounding. When the water was exposed to words like kindness, or to music such as a lullaby, intricate, delicate, beautiful formations resulted. When exposed to words like "hate" or hard rock music, horrific contortions were created. The most fascinating of all is when the water was exposed to the word "love," the ice crystals grew exponentially into the most beautiful artistic designs, far more intricate and glorious than any of the other crystal patterns created, and they kept growing and growing without end.

The human body is composed of seventy percent water; imagine how much of what is within us can be affected by something as commonplace as a word spoken or a tune heard. Our family has been fascinated by this scientist's work, so we continually remind ourselves that we want to create only beautiful crystals in ourselves and in others. When we make a mistake, we try to repair the damage by saying, "Okay, now you have to say two nice things."

*Happiness comes from within
but it begins from on high.*

CHAPTER THREE

Be Happy

THE DEGREE TO WHICH YOU LIVE THE GOSPEL

A good friend once told me that the "degree to which you live the gospel of Christ, is the degree to which you will be happy."

She said that she looked carefully at each of the people in her family and could measure, by degrees, the happiness each had in their lives. She said that it all matched up perfectly to the degree of devotion they had to the gospel of Christ, which is the "Great Plan of Happiness."

THERE YOU ARE

My brother often says, "Wherever you go, there you
are." I once had a friend who hated living in
Fremont, California, because she missed Utah. She
then moved to Los Angeles, California, and hated it
because she missed Fremont. Finally she moved
back to Utah and she said she hated Utah and
wanted to go back to Los Angeles.

If you are unhappy, you will be unhappy
anywhere. If you are happy, you will be happy
everywhere. Wherever you go, there you are.
Happiness is a choice.

ARKANSAS

When life gets particularly confusing and
distressing, I think, *I could move to Arkansas,
disappear, change my name, work somewhere
where no one asks questions, and life would be
simple.*

Then I say to myself, "So, are you in Arkansas?"
Then I answer myself, "No."

Then I tell myself, that if I am not in Arkansas,
then I have chosen to not go there. I have chosen to
stay right where I am. When I realize that the life I
am living is *my choice*, I then straighten up, quit

whining, and get busy with living my life in a happy, powerful way.

CHOOSE OUT

When we are deep in depression, and we are dragging up the past and seeing no hope for our future, choose out!

I have a cousin who would always say, "I'm out!" Over the years I figured out that he was making a choice of determination: happiness over misery.

It may take some effort, but we can do it; we are stronger than we think. Life is a choice. Faith is a choice. Church president Thomas S. Monson said, "Be of good cheer, your future is as bright as your faith."

CELEBRATE LIFE

Why bother even coming to earth if you can't celebrate life, and celebrate it often, with all the flair that "joy" encourages you to express. Eating chocolate, dancing, singing, and going to Disneyland are all for our enjoyment. God would not have invented some of these things we tend to avoid in the name of discretion and discipline if He didn't want us to enjoy them.

There is a time and place for everything: why do you think God invented Friday nights? And fine food? When you are on a cruise, you are committing a crime against God if you say, "Sorry, I am on a diet."

LIGHT THE FIRE

We all are damaged by experiences in our lives that leave us physically, emotionally, mentally, and spiritually damaged. We can light the fire under "Life is unfair; I didn't deserve this. I am this way because my mother or father did this or that." We can light that fire everyday of our lives and keep it burning bright, nursing and tending carefully all our hurt and our pain.

Or, we can take a big bucket of water and throw it on top of it and say, "I am done with that. I *choose* to throw away the matches. Instead of spending my time chopping wood and bringing it in through wind, rain, and snow so I can build a fire under my pain, I am going to use all that time and energy to build a new happiness. I will "unbreak" my broken heart and live life new and now.

Safe to Play

I was recently at a youth church event where everyone was practicing for an upcoming dance festival. All the youth and leaders were asked to participate in the rehearsals, even though only the youth were ultimately going to perform. Everyone was dancing except for the male leaders who stood in a long row at the back, by the doors. The young men were being rowdy and not participating. The girls and women, I noticed, were feeling a little uncomfortable. The rehearsal was a disaster.

I thought about why this happened. The men at the back were being perceived as policemen and as people who were not comfortable doing "silly" things that the rest of us were doing. What happened was created by how everyone was feeling: the boys were feeling like criminals because the men were guarding the entrances so the boys wouldn't escape, and the rest of us felt uncomfortable because we were being stared at and feeling like we were being made fun of in the minds of the male onlookers.

We felt "unsafe" by their lack of participation and the boys felt like bad boys who had to be guarded. The men needed to put away their guns and put on their tutus. That is how to make people feel safe.

I have seen this at parties where people will uninhibitedly join in a game, and but when someone declines, the whole tone of the party will then change because no one is "safe." Participating creates safety. By the way, the men put on their tutus for the following practices, and guess what? Magic!

SUNSHINE PEOPLE

Wherever they are, sunshine people engage whoever is around in conversation. They bring strangers together, if even for a moment.

I have a sister who is "brilliant" at this. When I am in a store with her, she has everyone talking and laughing together, sharing their stories and pieces of their lives. In the end, everyone realizes there is always some level of life to connect on. It is such a "warm" way to live.

LET THEM RUN

I love to see children run around the "church track" (the indoor corridors). I think they feel the spirit in their childlike enjoyment of the building. So much of what they experience in church is by sitting quietly in a chair. When they explode onto the track, I think they are expressing the joy they just learned about.

BE OF GOOD CHEER

On a table at a Relief Society gathering sat a little yellow card with a bee on it. Also on it were the words of our prophet, Thomas S. Monson, "Be of Good Cheer, your future is as bright as your faith." These words were able to sustain us through a yearlong family trial.

NO PEOPLE/ YES PEOPLE

Most people fall in one or the other category. There are times when we will need to move from our position of No or Yes to get to "happy" or "right" or "best." Be flexible in the pursuit.

SKIPPING

I have personally and scientifically proven that if a person skips, there is no way to be sad. It creates instant glee!

TEARS

Tears are a beautiful creation of God. They come when we feel the deepest joy and joyous laughter.

CELEBRATE

It is important to celebrate everything as big and brightly and beautifully as possible. It is good for everyone. It brightens the mind and heart. It creates memories that we keep forever and bind us deeply to those we love. People have to wait 365 days for their next birthday. That is not a long time for us—but it is for them! Celebration should be a way of life. We should look for every possible opportunity to praise God by celebrating every person and everything He made for our joy and blessing.

COSTUMES

I used to have a *Costume Room!* We moved and it became a Costume Closet. In the next move—black bags. No matter what, we have costumes! It has been a huge part of our family's life. We dress up to pick up someone from the airport, or at missionary homecomings, or 80s dance parties, etc. While living in Utah, when the college kids would have an 80s party at the house, they would tell people they didn't need to come in costume, because they could just raid our costume closet when they arrived.

All those who know of our commitment to costumes constantly borrow them. They are used at

Scout and Girl's camp, for manger scenes, plays, etc. I am always getting late night phone calls from desperate mothers seeking a costume for Halloween, or for a performance, or a church activity. It is very rare that we do not have what people need, and we either get them back or not, it doesn't matter, as long as the world is blessed and brightened by costumes.

One of my favorite memories is when I was making endless super hero costumes. At midnight, right when I was just finishing hand-stitching a hand-made logo I had created onto a stretchy shirt (while my son was wearing it), in comes one of his friends wanting a super hero costume. I finished it at three o'clock in the morning.

But, the ultimate favorite is that there is never a question of if my children will dress up for Halloween, it is only, "What are you going to be this year?" It is an absolute given, whether we are thirty-five, fourteen, or sixty. Yesterday, while my son Jack was assembling his costume, he asked, "Do you think everyone at high school will dress up for Halloween?" I said to him, "All I know, is that there is no way on earth Tommy would have ever considered going to high school on Halloween without one on." (Tommy was his older brother.) So off he went. I call it a grand "service to mankind." It brightens people's lives and makes them smile.

Jim and I walked down Santa Barbara State Street yesterday and loved seeing almost everyone in costume. We, of course, every year, feel it is our duty to honor Indiana Jones and Cruella De Ville.

The joining of hearts is the ultimate gift.

CHAPTER FOUR

Love & Marriage

I WISH I HAD A GIRL WORTH FIGHTING FOR

The subheading is the name of a song from the Disney movie *Mulan*. It describes an eternal principle. When a man marries, he becomes a real man. He has something to fight for, more to live for, and a kingdom to build for people he loves. He performs better in all areas of his life.

The God-given right a man has to provide for and protect a family is an eternal gift.

LOVE

Love is a choice. "I fell in love. I can't help it." That is a falsehood. You can help it. You choose who you love. If someone is not worthy to spend an eternity with, you can choose to not "fall in love with that person." We are not weak, helpless spirits that are being thrown around by every whim or fashion of our world. We are strong, pre-mortal spirits with divine missions to accomplish.

Choose to spend eternity with someone who will help you accomplish your mission. Choose someone whose mission you can help accomplish.

WE GAVE IT A SHOT

My husband and I have been married over forty-two years. There are some things that each of us do that are considered undesirable habits. A little while ago we stopped and thought about those things and decided that those things were never going to change. We gave it forty-two years; we gave it a shot. A "long" shot. Letting go of "socks on the floor" or "squished toothpaste" is a better way to live.

CAN YOU ENVISION YOUR LIFE WITHOUT THEM?

My sister-in-law asked her daughter this question when she was pondering whether she should accept a proposal for marriage. Her daughter's immediate response was, "Absolutely not!" There was her answer.

SEVENTY PERCENT

My friend said that when you are choosing your eternal companion, you should go for seventy percent of what you want—not one hundred percent. No one has it "all." We do not have it "all" ourselves. And the seventy percent of one person will not be the same seventy percent another person has, so decide which thirty percent of each person you can live with and give everyone a chance.

FORGET THE KIDS

I once scanned through a parenting book that looked interesting. If I could sum up the author's message it would be that the best gift you can give your children is a happy, solid marriage. He said to concentrate on the marriage, "not the kids." The kids will inevitably win our attention, but the marriage is the key. Give them your beautiful,

nurtured marriage as a foundation that will
"nurture" them all their lives.

ULTIMATE DATE

Sitting across a table with someone—at dinner,
over hot chocolate, or while playing a game—is the
ultimate date because you are looking into the eyes
of who you are with. Real connections can be made
and who people really are can be revealed while
sitting across from them. Whenever possible, avoid
sitting next to the person you are interested in
getting to know or spending time with. Always sit
across.

LOWEST THING

My Dad once told me that he believed the lowest
thing a man could ever do was abandon his wife in
her later years, for whatever reason, after she had
provided him with years and years of hard work
that had brought him a life of fullness, children,
memories, and joy.

IN-LAW

The people my children have had the privilege to
marry are my new found treasures. They are all
"what's not to like" beloved children of mine.

By watching over many years, I have learned what happens when the choice is to love or not to love in-law children. I have found that if you love them, you "get" twice as many children. If not, you lose your children along with your in-law children. It is one or the other.

Keeping your children is not an option—it's all or nothing. Imagine how blessed I am. By the time all my children are married, I will have twenty children!

LONELINESS

I once visited a woman whose husband had recently passed away. She told me that she would often go to the grocery store just to walk up and down the aisles to be around human beings.

PROM

Fanny's Dream, a book by Caralyn and Mark Buehner, tells the story of a farm girl who decided she was going to marry a prince. When she heard that the mayor was going to give a grand ball, she waited patiently in the garden for her fairy godmother to appear.

But the only one that appeared that night was Heber Jensen with flowers in his hand.

Heber said, "Well Fanny, I'm not a prince and I don't live in a castle, but I have one hundred and sixty acres, a little log house, and I need a wife who will work by my side, through thick and thin, sweat and joy, and be glad for good food and great company."

They worked the farm, laughed, washed a lot of diapers, and grabbed the baby and the twins and ran out of their house that burned to the ground when Davy stuck socks in the toaster.

Finally, her fairy godmother did appear to her in the garden and asked if she were ready to go to the mayor's ball to meet a visiting colonel. She told her, "No."

Heber, who was reading a story to their three sons, asked her who she was talking to in the garden. She told him it was her fairy godmother.

He said, "Oh, sure! And I'm the Prince of Sahiba."

To which Fanny replied, "Close enough, close enough."

I had a close friend tell me, after she had been married to her second husband for several years, that if she had to do it all over again, even though she loved her current husband, she would have chosen to put the time and effort that was required to build a new marriage and deal with the confusion and challenges of putting "yours, mine, and ours" together for the rest of her life, into her first marriage.

I call this "Prom." I think there are marriages that fail because someone still wants to "go to the Prom" after they are married. Some marriages never take place because someone decides to live their whole life going from castle to castle, to dance with Prince after Prince, or Princess after Princess.

Media has poured images of unrealistic living into our minds, which has produced the age of the Prima Donna and Prima Don. It is great to go on vacation, go out to dinner, have parties, dress up, and go dancing. It is when someone believes that is what his or her life should be all the time that trouble begins.

Building a marriage and family is the most exciting adventure God has ever given mankind. The chance to create something really beautiful is often destroyed by someone looking up at the castle and wishing that was their life, which ends up being no life at all—just a pretty dress, a tuxedo, and a corsage day after day after day.

And at the end of those days, where is the thirty-nine year wedding anniversary celebration with children singing "just for you" songs they have worked tirelessly to learn? Where are the rehearsed, choreographed, and costumed performances of sweet or crazy remembrances that have piled up over the years by a family that worked hard together as a team?

The house will burn down, the baseball will crash through the window a dozen times, and the five year old will go to church with no socks. Someone will get lost at Disneyland, and someone else will rub butter all over his body and swim in milk and Cheerios® that are covering the floor. Cars will crash, teeth will get knocked out, limbs will break, and a car will get stolen with all your children's Christmas presents in it.

You will drive a big, huge, blue van that has broken windows and smells like fish for years, and you will have a child ask if the whole family can pray for them before they take the MCAT or apply for a new job.

You will hear twenty people cheer every time anyone does "anything." You will watch what happens when someone discovers who he or she really is. You will watch a child find the love of their life. You will see a daughter willing to reach up to heaven to bring a newborn child into the world.

A big, bright, beautiful life is lived by people dedicated to one another who are not distracted by the castle on the hill but look right in their very own garden for the Hebers and Fannys coming over the hill with flowers in their hand.

Inherent in this trust from God
is the immensity of its importance.

CHAPTER FIVE

Parenting & Children

PRINCESS PRINCIPLE

My dad always made me feel like a princess. I could tell that no matter what I involved myself in, he thought it was great and that I was great. I believe it is the job of a father, particularly, to make his daughter feel this way.

POSITIVE REINFORCEMENT

I attended a course taught by Glen L. Latham, Ed.D, who was a professor at Utah State University. I was so impressed with his classes and his books (*The Power of Positive Parenting* and *Christlike Parenting*), that I decided to give a copy of these books to each of my children as a wedding present to help them on their parenting adventure.

The same quote appears at the end of every chapter in his *Positive Parenting* book:

> *Research has shown that the most effective way to reduce problem behavior in children is to strengthen desirable behavior through positive reinforcement rather than trying to weaken undesirable behavior using aversive or negative processes." (S.W. Bijou, The International Encyclopedia of Education, 1988.)*

This quote and these books have blessed us all.

Hip

The only parenting advice I remember from my mother is, "Set your children on your hip; wear them on your hip for two years and saturate them with love."

"If"

Glen L. Latham's book, *Christlike Parenting*, discusses the importance of starting every consequential statement with the word "if." He wrote that this positive approach would completely change the interaction.

The statement, "You do not get to play with your friends until you finish the dishes," changes to, "If you get your dishes done, you will be able to play with your friends." The child is able to feel much more positively about what he is about to do and is therefore able to do his task with a happier, more positive attitude. He ends up feeling much better about himself and his parent.

The key is to remember to start your sentence with the word "if."

IF YOU PLAY WITH THEM, THEY WILL LISTEN

Children are much more inclined to listen to you if you play with them. They will open up to you because they are in a relaxed, safe environment. If you play with them, they feel like you truly love them. They can interpret taking care of them as a duty, but playing with them is pure love.

CHILDREN'S CLOTHING

If a child likes what you are buying for him, he will wear it. If you buy something less expensive that he does not like, he will not end up wearing it. It will end up costing you more because it will never be used and you will eventually have to buy something else. Buying the right thing once is the "cheaper" choice.

PROOF OF PREEXISTENCE

When a child is born, their soul is revealed over time. The very core of who that individual is never ever changes. Who my children are at two years of age is who my children are at the age of thirty-four. We can direct and guide and work behaviorally with them, and we can put undue or uninspired pressure on them that can cause both parent and child pain, but God created who they are in the preexistence.

No matter what our efforts—good or bad—they are who they are forever. As you watch this constancy over the years, you witness countless evidence all through their lives that prove there is preexistence. The glory and uniqueness of the soul, so immaculately created, is a wonder to behold in and of itself. To witness its never-changing nature is beautiful proof that we lived with God above and were fashioned by Him alone in the preexistence.

Terrible Best

My husband and I often say to each other, "We were just trying our terrible best," when referring to our parenting skills over the years.

We ran onto the book *The Power of Positive Parenting* by Glen L. Latham much too late in life. We found ourselves reading the book and gasping in horror at all our mistakes. Now we give this book to each of our children as wedding presents, hoping that their "terrible best" in raising their children and our grandchildren will be better than ours.

Quick Or Slow

In the scriptures, we sometimes read that the Lord is "slow" to hear the cries of His children, and other times we read that He is "quick" to hear their cries. The key word is *children*: He always considers us His children and He tends us carefully and wisely.

Acknowledging His hand in all things requires us to have faith that how the Lord listens to our "cries" is the very best for us.

Absorb

To absorb the pain of a child is a sacred responsibility, privilege, trust, honor, and calling. God provided in a mother's heart the special ability to take on the anguish of her children. I believe it must be so. A mother must be willing to take this on because there is no one else. If we neglect to do this for them as children, they may need professional help when they are older. We should be there for them "along the way" to help them process all the things that their particular lives are exposed to.

It is often very difficult—the pain becomes almost unbearable—to feel the depth of their sadness or sorrow, but we must allow them in. We must be there for them. And we can be there for them in a way no one else can. It is a God-given gift and we must use it in their behalf for the midnight calls, disappointments, and frustrations. Children have to learn how to process so much in such a short time before they leave us; we must always be willing and available to them to "absorb."

Tag Team

I have noticed that parents have a natural inclination toward either leniency or a rigid approach to guidance and discipline. I have also noticed that it circumstantially flips back and forth.

When I am Tiger Mama at the helm, my husband generally takes a more relaxed approach, as if to say, "you've got this." When Tyrannosaurus Rex is on the frontline, I am able to take a back seat. It works as a "checks and balance" system in teaching and guiding, and in times of physical, emotional, or spiritual crisis in children.

I like the teamwork of parenting and I believe it is better, in the end, for the child to be safeguarded and blessed by parent tag-teaming.

NICKNAMES

I once read in a newspaper article that the reason we give nicknames to our children is because sometimes their name is just not enough to express in one word how much we love them, so we invent extensions or new creations to express that love.

TOP RAMEN SOUP

One night, my husband and I came home to a houseful of my teenage son's friends. The kids were running crazy everywhere, which is exactly how we like it, but my son was not. He was upstairs on an outdoor patio sitting on a swing with a girl.

Our son got up and immediately came downstairs. He was devastated by the assumption he felt we had naturally made about the two of them. He was sobbing uncontrollably and trying to get the words out that his friend was sick and he had just barely gone upstairs with the Top Ramen he had made for her. He said he had been there for a matter of seconds when we walked in.

What was so wonderful was his reaction. It was important to him that we knew he was a good boy and that he would never be in the situation that this seemed to be. It was a beautiful moment with our son. We all hugged each other. We were able to assure him that we never questioned him; we knew beyond a doubt that he always stood for truth and righteousness among his peers.

TEXTING

I used to know what my children looked like. I used to know the color of their eyes. But now I have forgotten because all I ever see any more is the top of their heads.

PERFECTION AT ELEVEN

Whenever we felt like we were expecting our children to be perfect at young ages, we would always say that we, ourselves, have so far to go. It takes a lifetime. We keep evolving. We are works in progress to the end.

Amazing Job on Me, Too

I went to a nephew's wedding lunch where friends and family gathered. When the bride spoke, she said, "I want to thank my groom's parents for doing such an amazing job raising such a great son, and I want to thank my parents for making me amazing too!"

We should all feel like that—like we are amazing! Our parents and God work very hard, all the time, so we can each feel like that.

Fishing Ties

Two sisters, whose father had recently passed away, were sitting in a boat together, fishing. They were arguing about how to make the ties on the fishing line. One said that Dad had taught her how to tie so that the fish could be released. The other daughter said her dad had taught her to tie so the fish could be caught.

They then realized that their dad had taught them differently because he knew each of his daughters: one would want to release and one would want to catch.

ANNIE

Annie taught me that the world still needs princesses. When someone asks me what Annie's personality is like, I remark, "Pink!"

Tea parties, high heels, tiaras, make-up, dress-ups, and dolls all bring about a world that should never be forgotten. You can feel the magic when the imagination of a little girl is full of fairy princesses and handsome princes.

There is a magical feel to the air where Annie is playing and everything feels like pink cotton candy. If only we could all go there for awhile...but even to witness it can be restorative and can enliven the soul or can turn everything pink again, which is exactly the color this whole world should be. (Written when my daughter Annie was two years of age.)

BIRTH

I like to show up after the birth of my grandchildren so the mother and father can experience their sacred moment, where heaven reaches down and earth reaches up to bring them their holy child. I believe the angels singing and the sacred mist that hovers over that occasion binds their hearts together in deep ways that are better left uninterrupted by all of us "anxious to see" loved ones who are standing on the sidelines.

WHO HAS THE HISTORY?

When a parent makes a decision for or counsels a child, they are coming to that moment with huge history behind them. They have been with their child since the time they were born. They watched them all throughout their life. They loved them, cried over them, laughed with them, spent time with them, prayed over them, dealt with them, and worked with them.

There is absolutely no one else on earth in a better position than the parents to make a decision or give guidance to their child. We should trust parental guidance and decisions; the yearning and praying and love cannot be measured, and it all comes into play at the moment of decision and counsel.

WHAT THE TENTH CHILD TAUGHT ME

Our tenth child Jack taught me that the "human experiment" works! He was born when I was forty-six years old, and by that time we just wanted to have fun with this gift from heaven. Everyone adored Jack from the very start. My other children said that the very best thing I have ever done in my whole life was to bring Jack into their world. Everyone wanted to play with him, and be with him. And because Jim and I were, by now, entering into our grandma and grandpa mode of living, we were more inclined to enjoy Jack than parent him. We raised him as if he were a grandchild; we gave him everything he wanted and let him do everything he wanted, and it was so much fun!

Jack would just sing all day loving his life, and why shouldn't he with all those adoring people around him? I remember one time at dinner; he was not happy about what we were eating so we took a gallon of ice cream and set it on his plate. We let him eat straight out of the carton. How about that for bad parenting? But what a life for Jack!

My older son Jimmie said that he would have to save up his money for weeks to buy one G.I. Joe®, and every time I would take Jack to the store, he would come back with a new toy. It was true; I was doing what any good "grandma" would do.

Thankfully, Jimmie lived with us for a while and he was often a real parent to Jack. He would take him on field trips and had the energy to do all sorts of things we had grown less inclined to do. The result from our human experiment is this: all the mothers in the neighborhood want Jack to play with their children.

My next-door neighbor recently said to me, "How come when Jack comes over I just want to kiss his face off and when the other neighbor kids come over, I get upset and nervous and want everyone to go home?" She has also told me that he is always wonderful with her autistic child when other children try to exclude her.

Jack gets on his bike and goes from house to house blessing everyone's life with his happy spirit. The mothers say that he is always singing and that their children are learning all kinds of songs ranging from primary songs to rock songs. So what I have learned from Jack is to enjoy your children, spoil them as much as you possibly can, and let them sing their life away.

When I stand back and take a serious look at why Jack "worked," it was because we had spent so much time truly parenting the first nine children with all our heart and soul (doing what we call "our terrible best"). The patterning for how to behave and how to live life was daily ingrained into Jack's heart and mind by his other brothers and sisters. He reads his scriptures every night because they always have. He brushes his teeth because they do, etc. He never seems to ask for or want much, I believe, because all his emotional needs are so "overfilled" by all the love that is poured into him by his brothers and sisters who are old enough to appreciate the joy of their new brother. I wish every single child that is born on the earth could be raised as a tenth child in a relaxed, loving environment where everyone in the whole family appreciates the gift of a life. Jack was born to bring joy and he has done just that.

It's Everyone's Business

I have a dear friend who has been a nanny for most of her life. She is very interested in the welfare of "little ones." If she notices a child being physically or emotionally abused in public, she will approach the offending parent and tell them to stop their behavior. The response she usually receives from the parent is, "It is none of your business," to which she replies, "It is my business; it is everyone's business."

Children are a gift from God on loan to us as parents. How we treat His "little ones" is certainly His business and should be ours also.

OUT OF THE NEST

I recently passed a young mother in a parking lot who was carrying a brand new baby. One little girl was hanging on to the mother's shirt and another little girl was hanging on to the mother's pant leg. Then, trailing behind the group was the oldest brother, who was also very young. I saw that the brother was crying. He all of sudden yelled, "I hate babies!"

I felt badly for him and thought about how each child has to, inevitably, be "kicked out of the nest." Whenever a new child was introduced into our home, along with the excitement and celebration, there came an accompanying sadness in the one who was no longer on Mom's lap, and heartbreak for the mother who knew her "young must learn to fly."

One day I woke up and looked around me. Our newborn child was at my side, and another had crawled in during the night and was by my other side. Then I noticed there was another child above my head and another at my feet. The last child just climbed on top of me. I imagine I was tired enough to not have noticed what had been happening. At that moment no one was out of the nest. I wish it could always be that way.

JUST A CAR

When I was sixteen, I crashed our brand-new car into our family station wagon. I went to tell this to my father, who was lounging around the pool with my family.

He calmed my tears and told me to not worry—"It is just a car"—and then he didn't even get up to go and look at the damage. He wanted to make extra sure that I knew I was more valuable to him than a car.

IF THEY CRY THERE IS A REASON

I have never been able to let my babies "just" cry. All my life I have been exposed to opinions, spoken or written, about how "crying at night" helps babies get used to sleeping through the night, at naptime, or in times of distress. I do not believe a parent should deprive little ones of feedings and other forms of care to achieve a goal, heralded by many, that can cause psychological, emotional, physical, or mental distress or trauma.

If a baby cries there is a reason. A child has limited options. Regardless of what the problem may be, the form of communication between baby and parent is singular—crying. I often find it hard to sleep at night. When I have a bad dream, I get up, walk around, and say to myself, "It wasn't real," until I believe it. When I am hungry, I make toast. When I am uncomfortable, I roll from one side to the other. When I can't turn my brain off, I read. When I am in pain, I take medicine. When I itch, I scratch. When I am lonely, I snuggle up to someone I love. When I am depressed, I ask people who love me to listen to me. When any of these things happen to a baby, they cry. Until a child is old enough to make it "their job" to take care of these things, it is "our job."

I do not believe that a tiny infant, or even an older child, is trying to fiendishly manipulate, control, or enslave a parent by expressing their needs or wants. I believe that children have real needs and wants—real ones. Their cry is their voice—their only voice.

My own experience: My husband and I were required to travel for his business for a couple of days. We left our child, who was a little under one year of age, with parents we trusted. When we returned they told us that our child cried the whole time we were gone. They said they finally laid him in a playpen and "just let him cry" because they didn't know what else to do.

From the moment of our return, our child glued himself to my body and "soul." He literally needed to be next to me every second. When I would drive, I would have to set him as close to me as was possible. When I would cook, he would be on the counter, cracking eggs open for me. If we were in public, he wanted to be right by me and did not want anyone talking to him. For his emotional security it was required that we become one person. Of course, I loved this. He was my precious partner.

When he was born, the immensity of my joy over him exploded into my heart and this chance to keep him close fit perfectly with my delight and overjoy in this gift-from-God child. I have always loved my mother's advice to "wear your babies on your hip for two years and saturate them with love." This was not just a good idea; in this case, it was a necessity. It was a necessity that was a great privilege for me.

This child grew quickly from this place to one of joy and confidence. Together, we opened up our world from "on my hip" to his taking on the world to become a brilliant man of great contribution. And while he has become a confident person in many aspects, he has told me a few times that he has struggled to sustain his attachment to people in various contexts.

Imagine the fear of suddenly being away from the familiar arms of his mother, taken to a foreign "land" (an unfamiliar playpen), being deprived of the love and care and perhaps even the physical nourishment needed, and having no evidence that his present situation would ever change. It must have felt like a hopeless eternity in the dark.

Fear is the outcome of unmet needs and wants in a small child. Making a small child secure by meeting his wants and needs, at a very young age, relieves the fear and allows the child to be able to devote his life to learning and growing. He does not have to devote all his attention to wondering if someone will come as he lays there, completely helpless on his back, waving his arms and legs around, crying. He knows his mother or father will always be there for him. He then can stretch and work and learn and laugh and become a child of wonder and joy, relieved of the burden of fear—full of faith in a bright future.

Love is the answer. How can deprivation of love in the form of withholding the care we should give be the answer? Despite all the literature or talk show opinions or fad-parenting ideas, there is not one person alive that doesn't know, deep down in their soul that letting a child "just cry" is wrong. I have heard of mothers going to other parts of their homes, curling up in a corner and plugging their ears—crying—trying to adhere to the newest, most popular idea being circulated among new mothers. God gave our children to us, not to "them," and not to "their" ideas. He gave us the keys to raise our children. We should trust our hearts, listen to our own inner voice, and listen to God. Every child has different emotional and physical needs. The freedom that comes from trusting yourself and God while you raise a child is a liberation of the heart and soul that can only bless the lives of your children and family.

If they cry, pick them up. Look into their eyes. Listen to your heart. You will discover your child's voice speaking to you. You will hear and respond and be able to raise a secure, loving, and happy child.

FAITH AND FULLNESS

I pray that my children will live lives of faith and fullness. It seems that "fullness" just naturally follows when we "look to God" and live. Everything seems to "blossom" before our eyes.

Friends are family.

CHAPTER SIX

Friends

ALL MY FRIENDS

My daughter said that all her friends who went astray began by swearing.

NOT RESTRICTIVE

My son once told me about his friends who were telling him that his religion was too strict. He said to me, "It is not restrictive; it is protective."

WHAT WE LOOK LIKE

I have a friend who always looks like a painting. She is and has gorgeous...everything. When I first met her, I went home and told the family we had a movie star living in our neighborhood. I told her that what she does is a gift to all of us, because what she does with clothes, hair, makeup, and jewelry, etc., is absolute art. And it gladdens our hearts and eyes when we see her.

I thought about how we dress nicely to go to church—out of respect. I believe we show respect to others by presenting ourselves nicely "to the world" everyday. When you think about it, we don't really see ourselves all day. We are "behind" ourselves. So how we look is really a gift to others, and it shows respect. It says I care about you enough to look my best for you. It is similar to setting a nice table; it tells your family you value them enough to make things nice for them.

PARTY'S OVER

My son says that as soon as you turn on the television when you are having a party—the party is over. Everyone starts to disconnect. People make an effort to come together so they can be together. Provide for and allow them the opportunity.

WHO YOU ARE

I watch my friends and see...

One is deeply in tune to the needs and sufferings of others. She rubs lotion on our hands when she sees us, covers those who are cold, and works to create magic moments for the needy.

One is quick-witted, smart, and calls things just as they are, which makes us laugh, or ponder, or sing.

One is the embodiment of art that is all color and light flowing from her; it gladdens our hearts and beautifully frames her "through the fire" heart of pure love.

One sees us as God sees us and opens her heart to the magnificence in each of us. She reminds us that we are the "real" movie stars "moving" around here on earth and becoming famous to a heavenly audience.

One is flowers and lace and laughter and dancing.... Everything that is "bright" is within her soul and all she creates is similarly filled with light.

One breathes out beauty: it is the air within her artistic soul, which showers all she sees, all she touches, and all she knows. She is every color—but mostly gold.

One looks inside and can see all your soul. Then hand and hand with God she heals every broken heart.

It's just who you are.

VINTAGE

I have friend who works as a professional counselor. After coming to terms with and overcoming an immense emotional trial, someone she worked with said that, "she was still valuable; she was just 'vintage'—tried and true and more glorious for the 'wear.'"

THESE PEOPLE

When my mother passed away, we attended her funeral in another state. We came back to find our friends (people who had never even met my mother) planting flower and herb gardens, weeding, mowing, hedging, mulching, and cleaning in our yard. They were expecting us to arrive the following day but we caught them "in the act."

I keep asking myself, whenever I see such love before my eyes, "Who are these people?" My heart keeps answering over and over again, these are people who love the Lord so much they cannot be held back from expressing it and showering it out upon all they see. Who are these people? They are children of God.

GOOD BUT NOT GOOD ENOUGH

Cell phones, smart phones, texting, e-mail, Facebook, Twitter, blogging—technology has connected us in so many wonderful ways we could never have imagined even a few short years ago. We have found lost friends, made new friends, and shared our lives with people around the world. The ways our lives have been enriched and expanded are immeasurable. It is all very, very good—in fact it is greater than great.

It is still, however, not good enough.

I have had a philosophy of life that is a subset to Circle Living. It is called "sideways" living. We often find ourselves sideways—sitting in a car, in a movie, at church, at school, on a subway, bus, airplane, etc. These are inevitable necessities of our reality.

This is definitely not good enough.

Because of the "wonderful" and because of the "necessary" we must always be looking for opportunities to get in front of one another.

When my husband and I go out on dates, I always tell him that at some point in the evening I need to sit across from him and talk to his eyes.

We need real live people in our lives to make ultimate connections. I stood in front of my mirror, at midnight, recently, and said, "Karen you have lived here an entire year and you have not made one friend." I had lots of friends, but not people I regularly spent time with. I had been busy with endless family connections, but the friend "place" in my heart was feeling vacant. So the next day I called someone up, who had invited me to walk with them, and told her I was going to be one of their new "walking, talking ladies." It was like magic. Real people friends were in my life, and even though we were doing a lot of "sideways" talking, we would also, at times, stop and talk with our eyes.

You can see why I am so excited to find the women who stand in the mirror at midnight and wonder what is missing. They are all of us. Many of you are involved, already, in circles that have become immensely valuable to you, or have even become your lifeline. You are in book clubs or other regularly scheduled events that bring you together. When I talk to women who are involved in Circle Living, they express how important it is to their life and they "wouldn't miss it for anything!"

Let the Story Live

When a friend is telling you a story about "one" cracked tooth, do not follow it immediately with your story about "two" cracked teeth. Let the storyteller have their moment. Even if your story is more fantastic and you are exploding with fifteen teeth stories, hold back and let the moment become alive for someone else. Someday, when the time is right, you will have a perfect situation where the "two teeth" story will have its day in the sun.

Motherhood is a new day dawning
that never allows the sun to set.

CHAPTER SEVEN

A Mother's Love

MOTHERHOOD

Motherhood is an eternal condition that is confined to the restrictions of mortality. The opportunity for bringing children to earth fades away as the body ages, but the longings for continuing motherhood are deep and eternal.

When I had nine children, I was in the middle of a conversation with my mother-in-law and said, "I think this is going to be my last child." When I said these words, I was surprised at the reaction to my own words. I began weeping, almost to the point of hysterics. I cried for half an hour before I could regain my composure.

Upon examining this behavior, I came to the conclusion that when mortality "smacks up" against eternity, it causes a painful reaction. There is something beautiful about the pain, because it is rooted in love.

NURSING

Being able to sustain life is sacred.

NOT GETTING SOMETHING DONE

I once heard a friend of mine say that she didn't want to have any more children because it keeps her from being able to get anything done.

"Anything done."

I believe raising a child is the greatest form of "getting something done."

KIDNAPPED IN RUSSIA

A missionary who returned from Russia said that when he was at his lowest point and was convinced that he was going to die, his final thought was, "I wish I had taken the trash out more often for my Mom."

WALK THE HALLS

As I was raising my ten children, I made sure I was always at church. It was hard to always "walk the halls" for three hours every Sunday, rarely ever hearing a lesson or a talk. My husband was often traveling, so I was often by myself with the task of keeping small children happy at church.

One day, when I was in the halls with several small children hanging on me, I told (yelled at) the Lord, "I better get something out of this. This is really, really hard and I am always, always here, so I want something really good to come from all this."

Several years later, I again found myself "walking the halls," and a strong impression, as clear as a voice, came to me and said, "What you will receive, is that all your children will be true to the Lord all their lives." I immediately found myself weeping.

The next thought that came to my mind was, "I would walk these halls for ninety years to have that blessing pronounced upon my children." So whenever I see young mothers in the halls, I encourage them to "keep walking." Nothing is more worth it.

TIGER MAMA—STAND ON THE PORCH

My husband calls me "Tiger Mama" to describe how I feel about anything or anyone that might try to "destroy" my children. I have always envisioned myself standing on the porch, sword in hand, proclaiming to the world, "You will not get my children."

FORTY-SIX YEARS OLD

If you have a child at forty-six years of age, do yoga during the pregnancy. That's my personal advice.

IF IT WORKS, DO IT

My dad was staying with us when our first child was born. He was watching me as I was struggling to figure out what to do as a new mother. He then gave me a piece of advice that I have valued all my life. He said, "If it works, do it!"

PROMOTION

In a movie, a woman is discussing her recent "move" from a career outside the home to being a stay-at-home mom. The man she was talking to said, "Oh, you got a promotion!"

That is how my husband has always viewed my motherhood. He often reminds me that I am doing

God's work, "to bring to pass the immortality and eternal life of man."

NOT YOUR CHILDREN, OUR CHILDREN

I was praying in my closet about my children. I was so filled with concern and yearning for their welfare and safety that my soul was stretched out in pain and agony with the weight of trying to do all I could to protect and save my children.

As I was begging an answer of the Lord to my question, "How can I save my children?" I heard the words (not audibly, but in my soul), "They are not your children; they are our children."

As soon as I internalized the power and spirit of these words, my agony was released and I felt not only a peace, but also a power. I knew that the Lord and I would together "save" our children. They were not "my" sheep, but they were "our sheep."

Knowing the power of God was to be with me as I worked to nurture and protect my children released me into a sea of faith, hope, and confidence that has changed my life forever..."for He is mighty to save."

Laundry: A Spiritual Experience

After years of mothering, I was in the laundry room pondering upon the work of motherhood. I realized that cooking and cleaning and doing laundry could end up being a spiritual experience if I really thought about what I was doing. Because I was willing to do these things for my loved ones, they were able to go out into the world, dressed, fed, and ready to develop their talents and accomplish their mission on earth. It cast a new light on my work.

Don't Keep Track

Mothers are often very careful about spending one dollar here, or a couple dollars there. Money goes out for a movie or swimming, for ours and for others.

I am of the opinion that as we raise our children together in a neighborhood, with all the comings and goings and shared outings, if we kept a perfect record of all we had spent on each other's children, it would come out exactly even in the end. It is so much easier if we don't keep track.

Bubble

I tell my children that whenever they talk to me, we are in a bubble. They are allowed to say anything they want to me in this bubble. They can scream and yell about all the crazy and horrible things in their lives. They can rant about who they hate, who they are mad at, who they are in love with, or just go on and on about nothing. It just stays there in the bubble. And it is great because I always know that they never mean any of the things they are saying.

For instance, when my daughter says, "I devote my entire existence to my children and they throw remotes at my head and yell at me all day..." I know what she is really saying, "I love my children with all my heart, but today motherhood is no fun at all and it's really hard. Yet it is what I want to do and I am so grateful to be their mother."

She and I both love that we have the bubble. We always end up laughing after all the exclaiming. It is very therapeutic, and the privacy of it allows for freedom and safety.

WHAT OPENS THEIR HEART

When I need to talk to my children about something really important, I think about where I should talk to them, and when I should talk to them.

I have a daughter whose heart is completely open when she is at the ocean. It calms her soul and brightens her spirit like nothing else can. Discovering where this place and time is for each child is worth all the effort.

SITTING PRETTY

One day, I was talking to my daughter about how truly unhappy I was that my mother had passed away. I was upset that I could no longer be with her. My daughter said, "Mom, you don't have to worry about Grandma; she is 'sitting pretty' up in heaven."

Immediately, an image of my mother came to mind. She was not just "sitting pretty" because she had raised a righteous posterity; she was actually "sitting pretty" among all the flowers she loved so much while here on earth. She was smiling as her blond hair flowed in the wind.

CHIPPING OFF CHEERIOS

At the age of fifty, I'm under a kitchen table still chipping off dried cheerios. What a good way to live.

COLOR

My mother was an artist in every sense. She expressed the art of her heart at every level of life.

Because of her, the art of the gospel has been of particular interest to me, which seems in perfect harmony with how symbolism is used to teach and enliven the mind, heart, and soul with the truth and light of the gospel.

Let me share a few lines from a poem I wrote for my mother's funeral:

She'll take us to her colored word
And let us see her life unfurled
A life of brightest color flow
She'll teach us why red poppies glow
We'll see now what she always knew
That skies were never gray or blue
She'll unveil to our eyes at last
All the treasure that God hast
The glories only she could see
The dreams we thought could never be
And when we close our eyes at night
She comes to us and blesses sight
Opens minds in visions bright
Takes us through her world of light

From all my years serving in the Young Women organization (through my church), I became fascinated by the colors chosen to represent the

Young Women values. I feel like each color is especially appropriate for each value.

- Faith is White—The color of purity in the faith of a child.

- Divine Nature is Blue—The blue of heaven's skies beckoning us to look upward to remember our divinity.

- Individual Worth is Pink—The color of love; the love that fashioned with care the uniqueness of each soul on earth.

- Knowledge is Green—The color of growth and the expansion of mind.

- Choice and Accountability is Orange—If there was a contest in heaven for "greatest creation ever," the orange (the fruit) would most definitely win. We can "choose" to "create" a life that will "win" us eternal glory.

- Good Works is Yellow—When we serve others, the warmth of the sun seems to glow in both the giver and receiver.

- Integrity is Purple—The color of a noble soul. And finally,

- Virtue is Gold—The color that life has taught me is the ultimate of all colors. This color is dear to my heart; this color is all my heart. I have watched this color play out in my life. This color is responsible for all that I treasure most in life. It is the color of the power of the atoning sacrifice of Jesus Christ.

We all know what black looks and feels like. This darkness is all the concern of our Savior. He went into the Garden of Gethsemane to gain the power to dispel all our darkness. The Father asked Him to enter the garden so that black would not be a color on earth. He partook of the bitter cup, He tread the wine-press alone, He shed great drops of blood, He showered the world with words of forgiveness from the cross, and He triumphed over dark at the tomb.

The power of this healing love born out of this sacrifice is what vanished this color from the earth and unleashed all the colors of creation upon all that He loved—all of us—and showered the earth with manifestations of His love in every flower, in every mountain, in every wave upon every shore, and in the brightened eyes of every healed soul.

Living life taught me how it all works. I remember seeing black when I opened my eyes. So I read yearningly, tirelessly the words of God in the scriptures and I prayed with all the energy of my soul. I opened my heart to the light of heaven and over time the light started to come back in my eyes—little by little—until one day I opened my eyes and I saw white.

But then there was a magnificent surprise; I thought white was the end, but something almost magical happened—even better than magical. I kept holding on tighter and tighter to the light and all of sudden I opened my eyes and saw gold. The Lord took my life from black to white to gold. It was a gold purer and more refined than any found on earth because it was paid for at a high and heavy cost. The price? The blood of the Lamb of God.

The words of scripture put to music by Roger Hoffman describe this process (paraphrased):

Consider the lilies of the field, how they grow.
Consider the birds of the sky, how they fly.
Consider the sheep of his fold,
He knows the meadows where they feed,
and He will heal those who trust Him
and make their hearts as gold.

Virtue is gold because it can make us brand new. When we become brand new, we are better than white—we are gold—because we have participated in the color of the Savior's sacrifice. If we push through the crowds and reach out to touch the hem of the Master, He will stop and look around and He will see who had the determination and faith to do all one possibly could to be healed. So we can hear Him speak the words: "I perceive that virtue is gone out of me." Virtue: the color of gold—the color we are when we are healed from black to white to gold. Virtue is so much more than the cleanliness of white; it is the power of gold in the royalty of divinity.

My mother was a great example to me of a woman of virtue—a woman of power. She was a woman who used the art of her heart to pour the light of truth into our minds, and the colors of values into our hearts, but especially the gold of Christ's virtue into our souls.

I know as we seek to embrace all that God offers, in all the colors of life, we will draw near unto Him, become like Him, and one day be with Him. God lives; Jesus Christ lives. Their love for us is a wonder to behold and we can behold it everywhere.

CROSSING OVER

When I was a young mother, I remember sometimes feeling like "I" was getting lost amidst the hard work and chaos of raising young ones.

I would reflect often on the "process" of becoming a mother and I finally realized, though it seemed like it was all at once, the "magic" began when I threw myself completely into the whole journey.

"I crossed over." It was no longer them and me, it was now "us," and we began developing our talents and creating our lives together. We did this with a new freedom—no tugs or pulls—just flow.

TEN IS EASIER

Raising ten children is easier than raising two. When there are two little helpless beings that basically cannot breathe in or out without you, you do "intensity mothering" every single second.

When other children join the family, every age adds help and benefits to all.

One gets the diaper, another opens the door of the car, another ties shoes, and another makes funny faces at the baby so she will stop crying. They can eventually babysit so you don't have to carry four napping children into the car to drive one of the children to piano. And then someone gets a driving license!

THE GREATEST THING YOU WILL EVER HEAR OR FEEL

The first time you hear your baby's heartbeat is the greatest thing you will ever hear. When you feel your baby move within you, it is the greatest thing you will ever feel.

FOUR HEAVENS

1. The first time I heard the heartbeat of my first child. It is the most beautiful sound I have ever heard...ever.

2. Getting up in the middle of the night with a little one—when everyone else is asleep—to behold, in the silence, the miracle.

3. Waking up in the morning to realize that, one by one, five children have crawled in bed with me: the baby on one side, a child on the other side, one at my feet, one above my head, and the last one on my tummy. No more room left. It was a morning to remember and treasure forever.

4. Sewing, on a hot summer afternoon in Seattle, at the top of our spiral stairs in a very small loft area and looking behind me to realize that, one by one, eight of my children have gathered together behind me, occupied

in various activities, because children just like to be by mommy and mommy just likes to be by her children. It is the gravitation of love.

WHO'S CHILD IS THIS?

When I was a new, young mother, I listened to all my friends' advice and read every book I could find about how to raise a child. My mind was so filled with what other people had to say that I lost confidence in myself and felt paralyzed.

I went to my husband with my dilemma and he asked me to whom the Lord gave this child. He said, "He didn't give your child to Connie or Beth or Susan, He gave this child to you. So He trusts you, not them, to be able to mother your child."

I felt the spirit confirm that the words he spoke were true and something happened inside me at that moment—freedom! I felt free to explore my own heart, mind, and soul for the answers to how to raise my child. Since each child is so unique, it has been a blessing to realize that you can trust what you feel inside as the source to determine the right thing for your child. The Lord gave the child to you. He trusts you to raise this child.

What's a Life For Anyway?

Wilbur, the pig, had a devoted spider friend who wrote in her web the words, "SOME PIG—TERRIFIC—RADIANT—HUMBLE," which opened the eyes of his animal friends to declare he was, also, phenomenal, wonderful, and unique. Wilbur, the runt of the litter, told Charlotte he did not feel like he was terrific, but she said, "You're terrific as far as I'm concerned. I think you're sensational."

How many times have our children's eyes looked up into ours, in despair, and said, "I am untalented, unattractive, worthless, the runt of all of God's children that have ever lived on the earth." And there we stand, with their hearts in our hands, with the sacred chance to bring them to a place of safety where their feelings will not be misinterpreted, but held, valued, nourished, and carried across their personal gulf of discouragement to a place of hope and eventual rescue.

It happens over and over again, a child's need to find a safe harbor, a Wilbur's barn, their mother's heart, where blinking, shining lights flash and ultimately glow and penetrate their troubled souls with words that say, "You're remarkable, you're magnificent, and you are definitely "SOME PIG!"

One of the most important discoveries I have made in my personal journey through forty-two years of mothering ten spectacularly different children is the "art of absorbing." It is the God-given ability to stand before a needy, desperate child and absorb their pain and frustration. I believe God fashioned a mother's heart in a very unique way, with a special capacity to create the safety in a barn that allows a child to look up, and see and learn that they are indeed terrific—at least terrific. The chance to be Charlotte to our Wilburs is a calling of the most sacred kind.

Our story ends with Wilbur working very hard to live up to all that Charlotte believed him to be and he eventually became all her webby words and won a special prize at the fair. As Charlotte is about to die, Wilbur says, "You have saved me, Charlotte. Why did you do all this for me?" She said, "I wove my webs because I liked you. After all, what's a life for anyway?"

The Family has won First Place from the beginning of time for "Best Invention Ever."

CHAPTER EIGHT

Family Relationships

BEST INVENTION

The very best invention that has ever been made is the family. A family of people who love you unconditionally and are committed to your welfare and happiness for eternity is an invention that wins all. And it wins all for us.

"WELL, DON'T"

After an altercation between two daughters, one sister was explaining her disappointment and exasperation at her own personal behavior and wondering what to do so she could gain more emotional discipline.

The other sister replied, "Well, Don't!" We should be able to "make ourselves mind ourselves."

EVERYONE STAY HOME

One day, everyone in the family was upset, all at once, because everyone had somewhere to go at the same time and nothing was working out: people couldn't get rides, things weren't ready for them to go, etc.

They all went to Dad and were emotionally describing their dilemmas. My husband stopped, thought for a moment, and said, "I know, let's all stay home."

Everyone stood, surprised, in complete silence; no one had ever thought of that as a possibility. So we all stayed home and had a great time together. It was a perfect solution for that particular evening.

SEND OUT

I came home one night after a day in Disneyland feeling absolutely terrible. Things had happened that had left me feeling overly monitored and micro-managed, and I was upset that a day I had looked forward to for so long sort of ended in ruins.

I was lying next to and talking to my adult daughter that evening, and she was similarly frustrated. As we were sharing, tearfully, I remembered a scripture I had just read the night before. I took out my *Book of Mormon* and I read the following from Alma 41:14-15:

> *Therefore my son, see that you are merciful unto your brethren; deal justly, judge righteously, and do good continually; and if you do all these things then shall ye receive your reward; yea, ye shall have mercy restored unto you again; ye shall have justice restored unto you again; ye shall have a righteous judgment restored unto you again; and ye shall have good rewarded unto you again. For that which ye do "send out" shall return unto you again, and be restored.*

We felt the words soften our hearts into compassion and understanding, and we felt ourselves trying to discover "the story" behind why things happened. With or without the story, our hearts felt healed. The next morning, apologies were made and oneness was restored. That which ye do "send out..."

Night Brain

Sometimes, when I would talk to my children late at night as they were retiring, they would launch into "night brain" talk.

"I hate everything! I'm untalented, stupid, overweight, worthless, aimless, hopeless, useless, and unimportant. I hate my hair, hate my nose, hate my legs, and hate my clothes."

I would tell them that they only felt like this because it was late at night and there were "thinking tired." I told them that in the morning they would feel great again. They insisted, "No, this is real. I will always feel like this because this is who I am and nothing will ever change, ever!"

In the morning, they would get up, get dressed, feel wonderful, and run out of the house with their new "Morning Brain" telling them they can do ANYTHING and EVERYTHING!

Solving it "Boy" Style

I walked in on an argument about who was going to get the car that day—a son and a daughter were going back and forth about who deserved it more. Finally, my son stopped, stood there for a moment looking at my daughter, and then he attacked her, throwing her to the ground, tickling her and mangling her.

The argument was over—I will never know how that worked—but it was over and one of them left with the car.

LOAVES AND FISHES

During a year of financial crisis, we witnessed a miracle every Sunday. We always had cousins, roommates, friends, other relatives, relatives of friends, and random *anybodies* come to dinner. The most we had, I believe, was around fifty people, and we never knew who would be coming. So, we would just make food. And we always had plenty, somehow. To see this work during a time of "great famine in the land" for our family was another sign of "the hand of God in all things."

DISNEYLAND

My sister-in-law says that her favorite thing about going to Disneyland is waiting in long, long lines with her family. We have figured out how to beat the system and always get on rides without the wait, but she works to do the opposite. She likes going on days that are really crowded. She says the real *magic* of Disneyland is not in the rides; it is in all the wonderful interactions between family members as they wait together.

TOGETHER

My husband had to commute from Seattle to Portland for six months and he only came home on weekends. My brother said that he would never do that. He said he would take his family with him, at any cost or inconvenience, to have them with him. He does not like to be without his family.

My son recently asked if we could do this so we could stay in Utah and live in the home he is so fond of. I told him that this puts too much pressure on a family. Families, now more than ever, are delicate creatures, and are under attack from all sides. I told him I would rather live in a tent than put the family at risk. I said that being together was "everything."

I know there are times when this is impossible, but I believe it is worth every effort to give "the family" its best chance to survive and thrive.

TERRIBLE BEST

It might be terrible, but it is our best, and sometimes that is all we have. We need to honor each other's "terrible" and keep the channels of love and forgiveness wide open in our heart, both coming and going.

BUNNY BOX

When bunnies are born they must be kept inside a box. If they leave too soon, they will die. What takes place in the bunny box is crucial to their survival when they are finally ready to venture forth. Inside the bunny box, the bunnies are wrestling and "scrumbling" around with each other, growing stronger each day from all their interactions with each other. Children are the same.

Little ones, in the important, necessary confines of the home, wrestle, hit, bite, yell, steal, annoy, cry, pinch, tickle, play jokes on, chase, get angry, love, laugh, make forts, have secrets, sing, whine, etc., and the learning begins. It is learning that will one day enable them to open the front door of their house, peek out, take a step or two, and realize little by little that they are going to be okay in that big ol' world out there. They can go to school and know what will happen if they steal someone's pencil or include someone who is being excluded. They have already tried everything in "the box," so now it is not as inviting to be mean to someone because they are familiar with the consequences. They learned all that in the box.

The round bunny box, however, is the ultimate box. When you walk inside, all you see is circles. There are round dinner tables with discussions like, "Guess what grade I got on my math test today?" or "Can you come to my soccer game tomorrow?"

There are family members kneeling in a circle saying, "Let us gather in a circle and kneel in family prayer and thank our Heavenly Father for the blessings we all share." There are circle games being played, "Do you love your neighbor?" or "Signs," and people sitting in a circle, talking and learning how to live like Jesus Christ in Family Home Evening.

There are rings on the ring fingers of the father and mother who love each other and love their children. Daddy is twirling Mommy around in circles while they dance in the living room. The rounder the bunny box the better! We may start out in a bunny "box," but all those hard edges seem to get rounded off with the circle living inside, and what is left is a round bunny box "on a roll" along the pathway to heaven.

Bass Lake

For fifty years, our family has met every year at Bass Lake for a family reunion. There are now close to 150 people that come every year. We camp in tents all together in a huge campsite next to the lake. There is magic everywhere: a missionary fireside where returning and outgoing missionaries report; a devotional every night; a family triathlon; a talent night, family dance night, game night, and song night. We also take trips up the falls and to Yosemite, dive off cliffs, and engage in every kind of boating craziness imaginable.

But all of that is nothing compared to the real magic that underlies it all—the great hidden powers in what happens to the cousins as you watch them together. They bond in every way imaginable during all their antics and all through the week. The cousins all squish together in a big mass across the sleeping bags where they all sleep together near the lake and they each become empowered as they talk and share together all that they are. The cousins know all about what happens because they have seen what it has done for them over the years. They call it "Cousin Power."

The cousins talk about needing to get to Bass Lake to get the Cousin Power back in their life.

When they leave each year, they all go away fortified from the examples and strengths that they each have. The sharing they do at the lake allows them to go away strong and healthy spiritually, ready to take on the new year. There is this flow of endless love swarming them the whole time they are together.

My very favorite thing about the whole experience is when I look over at the huge spread of cousins in sleeping bags, all squished together at night, and I see all these little tiny lights all throughout the area. They each have a flashlight on so they can read their scriptures before they go to bed. Imagine the effect of all those young people watching each other do this. Even my youngest, when he was two, was thrown in with the group. All ages are there—all those lights—it makes my heart sing. Just seeing all those *Book(s) of Mormon* getting "camped on" makes me so happy.

I don't believe any other type of reunion could accomplish what camping all together does. Not even in separate campsites. If you have hotel rooms, you separate and come together here and there. When you are camping (and it has to be in tents) no one wants to stay in a tent all day, so everyone is out all the time with others, constantly wandering between each other's lives. It is so beautiful.

I am so grateful for this tradition and for what Cousin Power has done for my children. I know we don't always like to deal with statistics when we talk about the power of love and tradition, but out of the thirty-nine grandchildren that my parents have, every young man and most of the young women served missions. All that are married have married in the temple, and all have stayed true to the Lord. In my mother's patriarchal blessing it said that the work she would do on the earth for her posterity would be monumental. I see her thirty-nine grandchildren as that monument, and I know that Cousin Power helped create that monument.

INVISIBLE STARS

To illustrate why the concept of "who has the history?" works, I share this story. A while ago, while on vacation with two daughters, my son-in-law, my three grandchildren, and my ten-year-old son, I decided to take the four little boys to the park. As soon as we left the hotel room, I heard and saw explosive signs of physical and emotional distress— loud screaming and enthusiastic fighting. I stepped back inside the room and told their parents that I had no idea what happened and no idea how to handle what happened.

They immediately said, "Oh, he just stole his invisible stars." The parents immediately knew what to do. I thought, *Imagine if I had tried to handle what happened. There is no way I would have ever guessed that one of the boys had stolen the other one's invisible stars.* But their parents knew immediately and knew how to handle it because they "had the history."

GROWING FONDER HEARTS

The reason we are bound so tightly to members in our immediate family is largely due to the fact that we are "with" them. When a child comes into the world, the helplessness of the newborn child requires proximity of the most intense kind. The child's literal lifeline is the mother. The survival of the child, on every level of life, is dependent on that binding.

Children grow and learn in the nest of the family and are nurtured by one another. The world of the child expands as time passes and other relationships are introduced into their world. Friends become a significant part of their social development and friends that they are continually with become bound to them, to some degree, but seem to fade in and out of their lives. Family members remain the underlying constant throughout their life and our life.

When children become ready to embark on the journey of discovery that will lead them eventually to marriage, the time spent with those involved in that discovery process will be the determining factor in ultimately being able to make the choice as to whom to entrust their own life and the lives of their future children together.

Living closely together and spending time with one another is the secret to hearts growing fonder. When loved ones need to leave for short periods of time, out of necessity, it is necessary to take steps to regroup with significant time spent together and an increase of emotional energy to strengthen the relationships.

Friends who desire to remain close must make special efforts to keep those bonds tight by planning to reunite frequently. That social organism does not have the power to draw together that the family innately has within it. Growing fonder hearts is the most beautiful form of gardening and the family is the ultimate garden.

CLOSE

If we had to do it over again, we would have moved the entire family during the time that my husband Jim was building a company in Portland while we lived in Seattle. There was another time when we had to move from California to Seattle a couple of months before my daughter's senior year of high school ended. She stayed with a best friend's family, but later told me that in retrospect she would have preferred to move with the family and graduate from our new town's high school, just so she could have been with her family during those months.

I have mentioned that my brother would make his family come with him if he traveled because he can't stand to be away from his family for even a minute. Sometimes our kids have asked if we could finish out a year when we have ripped them out of their flowing, full of friends, Happy Land Life. I once pointed to a bowl full of apples on the table and said, "Wherever Dad's job is that can keep this bowl full, is where we will live." It was as simple as that. It made perfect sense, then!

In our early family years in Boston, our family suffered from a difficult commute. Since then, we have done everything possible to keep home and work as close as possible. When a Father gets home from work, there are only a couple of hours left in the day to have that treasured "finally we get to all be together again" family time. And then it's bedtime, which comes way too soon for building those precious memories in such a concentrated moment of all together time.

Family Happiness is measurably increased by work and home being close together. I asked a son-in-law if he rode his bike to work and he said he couldn't because it was too close. That is living Heaven before Heaven.

Over the years, we and our grown children have been able to create the magic and joy that "close by" can bring. It is worth all efforts made to shorten the distance because, in reality, we are shortening the distance between hearts that yearn to be together. It is a natural pull and push within every family member that aches "to be together again." Every door that opens up in my life literally opens up a door in my heart. I work to make sure I am right where I think a family member is going to walk in because, then, there they are again, right in front of me! Love comes rushing through the door and I get to capture it right at the outset.

A song in my heart from my youth sings a profound reality of life:

"I'm so glad when Daddy comes home,
glad as I can be,
clap my hands, and shout for joy,
and climb upon his knee,
put my arms around his neck,
hug him tight like this,
pat his cheeks and give him what?
A GREAT BIG KISS!"

We are all Santa Claus to each other. We are each other's "Star of My Life," "Light of My Life." I know for sure that quality time can only be created by quantity time. There are places in my heart that hold regret, but they have taught me to value closeness at all cost. Looking back on the huge expanse of life that is trailing behind me, I see before me the Happiest of Happiest Times looming out above the rest. They all have been when we have made the sacrifices and taken the time to create CLOSE, which grows CLOSE.

*Faith is the work of power to create
and it creates miracles.*

CHAPTER NINE

Abiding in Faith

ATONEMENT

If it "saves your life," it will save other lives. If you are able to repent and forgive, you will give a gift of "life" to all those people who are depending on you to make it through this life in virtue and nobility. Every soul who has been given to you to know and love will be affected by your every move; they will be impacted by your every decision to use the gift of love and power that exists in the atoning sacrifice of the Savior.

A son of mine was being seriously bullied at school. It was required that I intervene, and help was obtained for the child that needed behavioral adjustments. I watched how my son handled this problem that had been going on for some time. He never once was interested in any kind of punishment for his friend. He continued to be around him, roomed with him and other friends on a musical trip, and one day after school, I saw the friend standing with my son so that I could bring them both home together to put a costume together for an event they needed to attend.

It seemed that forgiveness was already woven into the fabric of the love he had for his friend. My son moved through this difficult period of time in effortless nobility.

TAUGHT FROM ON HIGH

I always pray to be "taught from on high." The Lord is the ultimate instructor.

THE LORD IS THE GREATEST MAGICIAN ON EARTH

If we were to combine all the powers together of all our culture's imaginary superheroes, it would all look quite ridiculous compared to the powers of God to work miracles in our lives.

He stands supreme—all powerful, all wise, all good—and our acknowledgment of His hand in our lives, in all things, is His simple hope. He literally can do "anything."

I STILL WANT YOU TO FORCE ME

My daughter told me that she would not attend seminary classes if I did not force her. I then asked her if she believed in God and in His beloved son, Jesus Christ. I then asked if she believed that:

- Joseph Smith restored the gospel of Christ in its fullness on the earth;
- The prophet speaks for God in this latter day; and
- All the programs in the church are inspired of God.

  She answered, "Yes," to all the questions.

I then said that she would attend whether or not I forced her, and she said, "Yes, but I still want you to force me."

PROPHET'S EYES

I always look straight into the Prophet's eyes when he is speaking in General Conference. Each time, it comes to me, powerfully and undeniably, that "he knows."

WIND

When I think of the forgiving powers of the atonement, I think of the wind. When you are forgiven, it is as if the wind carries the offense away, and you can't get it back, ever. You can chase after it, but it is gone. And so are the things you have repented of; they are gone with the wind forever.

MINDS ARE FIRM

"O all ye that are pure in heart, lift up your heads and receive the pleasing word of God, and feast upon his love; for ye may, if your minds are firm."

The Lord requires that we don't just "flop around" here on earth, saying "today I am depressed," or "that is just how I am, I can't change," or "I don't feel like it today," etc. The Lord says that we can have all that He hath—but we must do something to gain it and we must make an effort. We must have a firm mind and firmly root ourselves in gospel principles and living.

WHOSE VOICE ARE YOU LISTENING TO?

Whenever you think a negative thought about yourself, whose voice are you listening to?

The only true source of self-esteem is the Lord; if you listen, He will tell you how He feels about you and what your divine potential is.

The other voice is bent on your discouragement and destruction. Make sure you are listening to the "voice" that truly cares about you. Listen to the one that truly loves you.

TALKING WITH OTHER WOMEN

A newspaper reported a study revealing the differences between stress relievers in men and women. It said that sports are one of the highest stress relievers in men, and that the very highest form of stress relief for women is talking with other women.

This made me think immediately of the wisdom of our Heavenly Father in creating the Visiting Teaching program at my church. He did not create a similar program for the men, but He knows His daughters well, and knew He could take care of them through this inspired program.

FAITH

I have seen many books and media programs presenting a "new" idea of "putting it out into universe" and it will "magically" happen. The magic presented as a new discovery is a principle of the universe that has been available and in force since the beginning of time. Many different names are currently being given to this power and the source of this power. Yet it has been with us all along and is the first principle of the gospel of Christ—faith. We don't have to buy new books teaching us about this power. We can go to the scriptures and have the Lord, Himself, teach us how faith works.

I was describing how faith could be used in our lives to my young sons the other day. One son said, "I bet I never get an iPod." The other son talked about how he could never be happy where we were going to move. I told them both that these declarations are the killers of faith and will propel them toward not obtaining what they want because they have relinquished the opportunity to participate in the greatest power on earth—faith in the Lord Jesus Christ. It is faith that what is important to you is important to Him.

The Lord says that if we ask for a fish—He will not give us a stone, so if we offer up the "desires of our heart" to Him and explain why it would be important, the Lord will do everything to honor our energy and prayer of faith. That is unless He has a better plan. And then if we truly "acknowledge the hand of God in all things," we would want the better plan anyway because God is smarter than us and He knows what is truly best for us.

My daughter told me the other day that she really wanted/needed outdoor furniture so her family could enjoy being outside to a greater degree. They are "struggling students" and didn't feel they could afford such a thing. We talked together about the power of faith and how what is important to her is important to God, and within a couple of days, after praying diligently for "the desire of her heart," she had a beautiful set of outdoor furniture that she found for next to nothing. The age-old power of faith is real and available to all—always.

CHOICE
Faith is a choice.

CALLINGS
I have accepted every single church calling that has been extended to me throughout my entire life, except one. When I look back now, at all the ramifications—the lost learnings, and the lost experience that came from that one "smarter than God" act—it fills me will immense regret and an

undaunted determination to serve anywhere, anytime. I trust my all to His tender care knowing he loves me.

SUBURBAN

When my daughter was expecting her fourth child, she did not have a car big enough for her family. She told me that a car would literally have to be dropped out of heaven for them to be able to have a car, since they were still in their starving-student stage of life. Within days, a big, white Suburban was given to them. I have watched "money or miracles" play out in endless ways in all our families.

THE ART OF MENDING

I was reading the book *The Art of Mending* by Elizabeth Berg, and came upon a paragraph that I have treasured ever since.

> *My relatives still make fun of me for my love of things domestic, especially my Aunt Fran, who, whenever we visit, always tells me she's saved her ironing and mending for me. Actually, I wouldn't mind doing it. I like ironing. It's the physical equivalent of staring into middle space. I think it*

waters the mind, if you know what I mean. As for mending, I think it's good to take the time to fix something rather than throw it away. It's an antidote to wastefulness and to the need for immediate gratification. You get to see the whole process through, beginning to end, nothing abstract about it. You'll always notice the fabric scar, of course, but there's an art to mending: if you're careful, the repair can actually add to the beauty of the thing, because it is a testimony to its worth.

I had an experience that made me understand this idea personally. I have a favorite painting that I found while we lived in Boston. It is easily over one hundred years old and over the years has become all the more dear to me.

One day, someone was playing ball with our dog near the painting. There was a candle burning on the table below it. The ball hit the candle and the wax sprayed all over the painting, the furniture, and the wall behind the painting. I grabbed my painting and my daughter, who was standing in the other room, and dragged them both into my bedroom. Through tears, I looked up into my daughter's eyes and said, "Tell me it's a thing; tell me it's a thing."

She consoled me in her inspired way and we went on with the evening that involved a house full of relatives and friends.

Later that night when everyone was asleep, I brought my painting out and laid it on the counter under the bright lights. I then worked, for hours, to lift the wax off my painting and the antique frame that surrounded it.

Finally, I had done all that I could. I stood back and looked at it. It wasn't the same, but it was still beautiful. In light of what I learned about "the art of mending," the painting had become more beautiful, because now it had all the marks of my efforts to restore it, which was in the end, a "testimony to its worth."

I realized that this is what the Lord does; He looks at his masterpiece—beaten, battered, and bruised by life—and through tears of compassion, under the bright lights of His love, He works tirelessly. In the garden, on a tree to ultimate victory (His work and His glory), carefully, painstakingly peeling the wax away. And there we stand, tended and mended, and even more glorious. His work to restore us emblazoned into our soul as the ultimate testimony of our infinite worth.

*Extending your heart to bless another
does exactly that—extends your heart.*

CHAPTER TEN

Giving & Being of Service

YOU ARE HERE FOR A REASON

This is a quote from the movie, *Superman*. Each of us has a very particular mission on earth. We are truly here on earth for a reason...for many reasons.

LATE

Someone spoke of being late to church as highly disrespectful, saying that our meetings belong to the Lord.

I have been late many times in my life and it has caused many problems, not only for me, but for others as well. I remember being late to a youth meeting where my daughter was in a dramatic presentation. The havoc caused by her not being there was something I have always remembered. Being on time to absolutely everything is a worthy, noble goal worth all our effort. The message given by our ability to do this is, "I value you and your time enough to be on time to what is important to you." Certainly our church meetings are important to the Lord and our efforts to be on time show Him the respect He most assuredly deserves.

GOD'S

Everything is His. It is our privilege and responsibility to share "all that He hath" given us with every possible person we can, to brighten and bless their lives in any way we can.

NEEDED

My grandma Bessie, who was eighty-four years old at the time, lived with us for eight months while we lived in England. She would always get up at 5:30 AM with my three-year-old daughter to have breakfast ready for all of us. I told her I didn't want her to feel like she had to do this.

She said, "You know, when you get older, the greatest thing you want is to be needed." She spent the rest of her life, until her passing at age ninety-three, going from place to place, wherever she felt she was needed the most.

Fourteen Dollars

During a period of financial uncertainty, my son asked me to take him to the thrift store to buy clothes for the upcoming school year. He had earned money from mowing lawns.

At the store, he gathered up $14.00 of clothing. I told him I would pay for it, and he said no. I said I would pay half, then. He said, no, he wanted to do his part.

Shoulder

I was standing in line at a counter and could overhear a young woman explaining that her husband had just passed away. The woman behind the counter reached her arm out and put her hand upon the young woman's shoulder, and they both bent their heads down. They just stayed there holding on to the moment.

One small act. One small moment. One great healing.

No Money

I used to spend all kinds of money on my children's birthdays, Christmas, Valentine's Day, Easter, and other gifts. I just loved doing this. I loved it so much that it was really getting out of control. Then we had no money. All of sudden. So I had to think of what to do.

On Valentine's Day, I sent my children a picture with my child and me, together, and wrote a long letter beneath it about how much I loved them.

For birthdays, I made them pillows that I created out of fabric that looked like a picture of them when they were young. One year I made a huge, homemade picture book with a long poem that I wrote about their life.

At Christmas time we all made homemade gifts. We went all out trying to create the perfect gift for the two people to whom we were to give gifts. It was amazing to see what everyone came up with.

Everyone spent countless hours creating shower gifts and friends' birthday gifts. I began sewing things and drawing pictures and writing poems. I now realize that the real secret behind creativity is having no money. It has been a fun blessing for me in this way, and my children said that it was the best Christmas we have ever had. They said that my homemade gifts were their very favorite...ever.

CREATIVE OBEDIENCE

My son said that on his mission he created a motto for how he did his missionary work: "Creative Obedience." He said that "obedience with exactness" was limiting to him, so he obeyed creatively, which breathed much more life, love, and joy into his work. He said you could do so much more than you might imagine "within the bounds the Lord has set." When he obeyed creatively, his missionary work came alive for him and those he worked with.

I recently spoke with a tennis coach who, while on his mission, would play tennis with his neighbor on his preparation day. Because of his expertise, he was invited to play on South England's tennis team, which his mission president approved after consideration. His participation in this "creative obedience" brought the light of the gospel, through his developed tennis talent, to three families who joined the church from that association. I believe our talents, when developed, can be used in so many ways to bring the plan of happiness to others.

ESTHER

We will all have times in our lives when we will be like Queen Esther. We will look back at why we are where we are, doing what we are doing, and realize we have been saved "for such a time as this"—to save a soul or to save a people.

APPRECIATION

My husband and I were asked to take care of the very hyperactive, unruly young son of a friend. We agreed, but were somewhat nervous because we were young parents without much experience at the time. The morning arrived and we received a call that our help would no longer be needed.

The father said to us, "Now just think of the gift I just gave you. Today, all day, you will think, 'Wow, this is great. We don't have to take care of that crazy boy.' Look how happy I just made you!"

When something like this happens—like getting stopped by a policeman and having him just say slow down instead of giving you a ticket—your day is better because you will appreciate what has happened. In being stopped by the policeman, you have the appreciation of your day without a ticket; or without crazy boys, it makes you have a better day. It is funny how that works. I think it has everything to do with "opposition in all things."

Brain Chooses "Out"

I once forgot to attend an event I had worked for months to create and organize. It was at a time in my life when the pressures on every single level of life were outrageous, unfathomable, and far beyond humanly possible to process or endure.

I think when you are in "one of those times," your brain protects you from "exploding" by choosing, either arbitrarily or not, to let something go to save your life or at least your sanity.

Each gift has a tag attached that says,
"Use to Bless."

CHAPTER ELEVEN

Talents & Gifts

Your Style/God's Style

I believe that we each have our very own style, unlike anyone else's in the whole world. I believe God made us each exactly the way we are, for a reason. We should be true to who we are in all we do.

Our "style" in which we approach our lives will vary dramatically from all others. We should feel free to explore, bask in, and celebrate that style by living true to the way God made us. We honor God by living true to our "style."

Shakespeare said, "To thine own self be true, and it must follow, as the night the day, thou canst not then be false to any man."

NOBEL PRIZE

We should be less concerned about earning the Nobel Prize and more concerned with the kind of "prize" we will receive in eternity.

COLUMBUS

Christopher Columbus was quoted to have said that he had "joy and cunning" for his work. I believe the Lord blesses us with a natural joy and cunning for the particular labors that are given to each of us, uniquely, to accomplish our life's mission on earth.

ABILITY

In the movie *National Treasure*, one of the lines was, "For that which you have the ability, you also have the responsibility."

We each have natural inclinations toward doing certain things, or developing certain talents. We need to use them for the betterment and blessing of mankind. The Lord requires it and needs it.

EDIFIED TOGETHER

A favorite scripture of mine is from the *Doctrine and Covenants of the Church of the Latter Day Saints* (D&C 84:110): "that all may be edified together."

I love watching people, who by being true to who they are honor God by developing the talents that are uniquely their own. These are their personal gifts from God. It is a delight to stand back and watch the beauty of everyone bringing forward their "offerings of the soul" into a gathering of souls. The differences and variety in this gathering create a magnificent whole, and all are "edified" together. Perfect!

THE CHANCE

For many years, I have watched a friend of mine live with a magic wand in her hand. Everything she touches turns into the most beautiful, spectacular creations such as I have never seen in all my life. It is an obvious gift from God "to gladden the heart and enliven the mind." She is a real "fairy godmother."

Whatever it is that you may wish in your life, she shows up and touches it with her "wand" and *Bibbidy-Bobbidy-Boo* there it is; your dream come true. But it is better than anything you ever dreamed because her dreams for you are even more brilliant than yours. That's because of the love from which it springs.

I once told her that I knew all about her special gift, and she said to me, "No, it is just because I have the 'chance.'"

The chance. Imagine if we always took the chance to share our gifts with others as freely and beautifully as she does. Imagine...

FORMULA FOR WRITING TALKS

I believe that when you are assigned a talk, there is a very specific message that the Lord wants to deliver to the special set of people you are to address. You have a huge responsibility to not only say what the Lord wants you to say, but to use your audience's investment of time wisely. Count all the people you are going to speak to and then add up all of the minutes that each person is investing in you, and giving over to you to help them and to bless them. This is a large investment.

Then there is you; there is something inside of you that is very sacred. There is a message that no one else has. That message is what the Lord is looking for and one that no one else can give. You are like no one else in the world and no one has experienced life exactly the way you have. That is what the Lord is after when He asks you to address His children.

So, I have come up with a formula for tapping into what is sacred inside a person who is preparing a talk.

1. First, sit at the computer or in front of the paper you are about to write on.

2. Then, pray that the Lord will be able to use you as a pure and perfect instrument or vessel for His message. But it is more complicated than that. He doesn't just want His words spoken, He wants His words spoken after they have gone through your heart and spirit, so what comes out at the other end is a combination of you and inspiration. It is the Lord's will combined with all that is uniquely you. It is a glorious message created by you and the Lord working together.

3. After you have prayed for this to happen, Free Flow. Let all your thoughts just start flowing out onto the paper or into the computer. Just let it all come. Don't even think about the assigned topic; just let everything that is in your heart come out. Gospel topics are all so interrelated that the message in your heart will always go along with what you are assigned, somehow. It is

the core of your soul that the Lord is after. The discovery of this is an exciting journey and an experience that will bring you very close to the Lord as you become partners in this effort to bless His children.

4. After you have free flowed and you have your heart out onto paper, you can now get to work on another level. Take what you have written and start to illustrate it or strengthen it with personal stories, quotes, scriptures, and words from the prophets. I usually use at least one personal story, one scripture, and one quote from a general authority.

5. At the end, leave at least one minute to bear your pure, simple, and therefore, powerful testimony of Jesus Christ and His restored gospel.

If You Want Them to See Your Eyes

If you choose to be immodest, you have made the choice to be an object, not a person with a soul. You rob yourself of being seen for the glorious, talented person that you are. People are so distracted by what you are immodestly revealing that they cannot look into your eyes—they can only see body parts.

Do not rob yourself and them of the chance to be seen for all that you are. Cover up and let your light shine into another's soul.

GIFTS

Our God-given gifts are precious and unique to each one of us. These gifts are valuable to us (and others), and have been given to bless and serve and brighten lives. These gifts can be used for good or ill. If you watch your children grow, you see them trying to figure out how to use their gifts. They learn by degrees the effects of using them.

I have a "mighty" daughter who we have called "queen of the universe" since she was one year old. She has remained "queenly" all her life. When she was tiny, she would get her way all the time because everyone was afraid to cross her. She even demanded, "I'm the Queen" to three of her older sisters when they were playing "princesses." All the sisters immediately relented and gave in to her power.

Over the years, we watched our daughter try out her gift from God on the world. Over time, it truly became a "queenly" power. She blesses the lives of all by her undaunted devotion to God. She is powerfully *everything*: powerfully righteous, powerfully influential, magnificently bright, spectacularly entertaining, and deeply loving. Whatever there is to do or be in life, she does it with and "is" the essence of magnificence. What a blessing to watch her choices to use her gifts for good.

LIVE YOUR OWN LIFE

We have been designated a certain time and place for living our own lives. We care for our own children, we tend our own gardens, we wipe the tears of our loved ones, and we serve all those that come into our lives who were placed there by God for us to serve. God takes care of and loves the rest, just as He loves us.

He tends the heart of the lady living in a mansion as well as the mother in a refugee camp. He is there for all of us. We must never think that having "things" or living in a more desirable situation means God loves us more. He is no respecter of persons.

Life is messy. We never know when an "earthquake," spiritual or physical, will upset all of our peace. But whatever our circumstance, God is there is help us through the chaos of life. It doesn't matter whether it is physical, emotional, mental, or spiritual—wherever we are and whatever we are doing—He is there to help us through all that is part of our mortality. He is there at every turn of the roller coaster ride.

HAIR CRIME

A crime against God is committed every time my son Jack's hair is cut. It has been a family war since he was born. He has beautiful, thick, blond, sticking-out-all-over-his-head hair. "Bed head" as an art form. It was a gift from God—not to Jack (he never sees it), but to us, his family.

OH, IT IS NOTHING

Often, when complimenting another for a talent they have, you will hear the words, "Oh, it is nothing." That is exactly right. The talents that God has blessed us with don't seem as valuable to us as they do to others, because they come so naturally to us. They just flow from us.

My son is very artistically inclined, and all his life I have been pulling beautiful drawings out of the trash can. He would say, "Oh, that's nothing. Anyone can do that." The fact is not anyone can do what we are inspired to do naturally and brilliantly. We should value our gifts as much as others do. We should praise God for the opportunity we have to use these talents and gifts to bless and serve.

Passionate Ownership

I have found that when people "own" what they are doing, they are much more excited, determined, and creative in accomplishing what they are passionate about. When I ask musicians to perform, I ask them to choose their own music because it is always more alive and heartfelt.

There is a danger to be mindful of when people come to you with their new idea, or goal, or disciplinary quest: if you jump in with all your ideas and map out how you would do it or get too excited about how you can help them, you will see their excitement diminish because they have just been "robbed." Creativity is such a personal activity between God and the creator. Intervening too much may take the "wind out of their sails," Be very careful. There is nothing more beautiful than the newly excited, empowered mind about to set forth on a new adventure of passionate creation.

Found/Lost

You could drop my husband off in China and he would be able to get anywhere he needed to go; he has a satellite in his head. It is most definitely a God-given gift. I, on the other hand, get turned around in a grocery store; I can never find my car, and I am always, always "lost." When I feel comparatively inadequate in this area, I remind my husband (and myself) that he did nothing to earn his "found" gift, therefore he is not smarter than I am. I have other gifts. But then I have to remind myself that I also did not earn my God-given gifts.

IT HAS TO BE OUT

If you want to play the guitar, it has to be out of its case and standing ready to be strummed. If you want to become a cyclist, the bike cannot be hanging from the rafters in the garage, it has to be standing ready. If you want to be an artist, leave the paint and paint brushes out.

PALM TREES ARE GIFTS—GOD THINKS OF EVERYTHING

While looking out at the ocean, it came to me that the reason God lined the ocean landscape with palm trees was because the design would allow us to always see the ocean, without obstructing our view.

LIKES WHAT HE MADE

God really, really likes what he makes. I think He is absolutely delighted with each person he creates. I think He looks at each masterpiece and thinks, "This is going to be so great, so fascinating, so fun, so rewarding..." (Similar to how we feel as we watch our own children grow up.)

He gives us our own little "pile" of talents and gifts, and then allows us to use them in any way we choose to bless and beautify and serve. I believe He is not happy if we ever try to "live" someone else, because then we can't "live" ourselves. When we are true to ourselves we honor God. By exploring all the gifts He has given us and becoming who He wants us to be, we can fulfill our own, very specific, very unique mission on earth.

He wants us to breathe out all we are onto the world, into the hearts of loved ones, and upon all the lives we are privileged to be a part of. We have within us all we need to be all we can be, and it is the only way to fully bless and serve. We need to love what God made as much as He does.

BRIBERY

Some of the best money we have ever spent has been in the bribing of our children. I once paid a daughter a huge amount of money to sing in one of my Christmas concerts. She was resistant and she kept raising the price, but finally she said okay.

The reason I was so interested and willing to make this "investment" is because I knew she was on the verge of giving up singing and her voice was a gift from God that could not be wasted. Right then, I knew it was the time—at that moment—and if she did this concert she would always sing for the rest of her life. That was many years ago and she is still singing.

PERFORMING/OFFERING

I believe the difference between performing and making an offering before the Lord is very decipherable; both in the person who is "performing" and for the person listening or watching. You can feel the difference. Consecrating one's performance to God and making the effort to connect with His purpose and the possibility of bringing people closer to God is a sacred trust.

I think of each person in the audience and estimate how many people are there. I then multiply this number by three minutes (the average time for a piece of music, for instance, to be performed), and I think of the responsibility I have to use their time wisely. Imagine holding in your hands the "chance" to bring others closer to Him. When singers prepare for this moment by memorizing the words, there is a greater connection there: eye-to-eye and heart-to-heart. I feel that when this can be accomplished, through physical and spiritual preparation, it is like you are bearing testimony "with" God instead of just "of" Him. It feels deeper, different, more holy, and more wonderful. It is no longer just a performance, but rather a sacred offering.

BE ME

My brother once said to my mother, who was frustrated with him, "Mom, you think it is hard to live with me, but imagine what it must be like for me to live with me. I have to be with me all the time!"

This son, who had super-energy and lived fast and full, has grown up to be productive, successful, and fun. He is an amazing father, a great provider, and is admired by all who know him. It feels like he is living five lives at once.

I think people who have a hard time being "themselves" just need a little more space and consideration. Then we get to "stand all amazed" when they do figure it out.

RICH PEOPLE

All the wealthy people I know think that all that they have been blessed with belongs to God, not to them. I guess that is why they live so brightly, generously, and lovingly.

FEAR

I had a friend who made furniture. I asked her how she knew how to do this and she replied, "Because I watched my dad do it."

My dad was a professor who published books and other writings. He also wrote poetry. I love to write and I also write poetry. I believe it is because I watched my dad. I had no fear about whether I could or not; I just assumed I could because he did.

I think fear keeps us from developing our talents in unfamiliar areas. Faith, being the opposite of fear, should rule our future and give us the confidence to try or do new things.

SEVENTH WONDER

My daughter calls her sister "The Seventh Wonder of the World." Her creative mind is such that it staggers my mind at every turn. Everything she touches blossoms as if she has touched it with a magic wand.

My other daughter calls her "Magic Person." (I love it when loved ones can appreciate the magnificence in one another.) Here is some of the magic she has made:

- She comes home from college and in twenty minutes she has created an enormous tepee in the forest out of random pieces of wood; has dug a fire pit with logs around it; and has all the little ones roasting marshmallows and hot dogs.

- She then proceeds to create a ten-foot high wicker chair.

- When she is due to leave in an hour by plane for my son's wedding, she uses the bride's maid fabric in front of her and creates and sews, without a pattern (in just one hour), the most beautiful dress. It is prettier and more creative than any of the other dresses.

- My brother is about to sell his Jeep to buyers who are soon to arrive at his house. He discovers rodents have eaten through the top. My magic daughter finds some appropriate material lying around, sews a sunroof into the top, and finishes it before the buyers arrive.

- We decide it is time to bike on the beach, and by the time we put on our shoes and walk out, she has already loaded eight bikes on the car, gathered all the helmets, and is waiting.
- Literally everything she touches grows into radiant living. I look down at what she has been "doodling" during General Conference and she has drawn a picture of the Savior in the clouds with Minerva Teichert-type framing around it.

It is like this everywhere with her. God touched her precious mind in a way I have never seen. She is truly, truly a wonder to behold. When you get to experience someone like this in your lifetime, you can only praise God for the chance to see "Him" in them.

LOVE WHERE YOU ARE

We tend to love the stage of life we are in because there are wonderful things about each stage of life that we keep discovering. All life at all times is a gift.

THE NEW ME

Recently, I was thinking about an enormous trial I had endured many years ago. I thought about the person I was before and the person I became after, and I was fascinated by the realization that I preferred being the "new me." There is so much more depth to my soul and to all that I am because of what I have been through. I feel like there is so much more to give to others now, and that there is more "to" me and "of" me.

I am glad the Lord knows how to bring us along and fashion us so we are "fit" to perform our labors and accomplish our missions on earth.

SALEH

The song "Putting it Together" (piece by piece and bit by bit is the only way to make a work of art come to life) describes perfectly the last few months of watching Saleh, my son Jack's music theater teacher, put together a show that won a National Competition and personal award of Best Director.

I have had many chances to study her genius, year after year, as she pulls together twenty-eight rowdy kids from behind her piano bench to create music theatre masterpieces. The judges are always amazed when she walks out from behind the stage, where she is playing piano, only to discover that she is also the choreographer, producer, director, voice coach, and music director. The Saleh miracle has also attracted 120 students to arrive before school to be in a choir. Also amazing is that she never directs the students during performances. She plays the piano while the hundreds of different pieces and parts run like clockwork.

She trusts they can do it, and they do! The "Saleh Secret" is incorporation and validation. When students have ideas, she not only considers them but often incorporates them into the choreography. She carefully studies the personality and talent of each individual and breathes life into their unique abilities. Her devotion to her internal principles as she fashions her "works of art" is what liberates her students, and then the magic happens "piece by piece."

Saleh's vision brightly beams before her at all times, and as she "lights" up each student by giving them their "chance," all the lights combine. If you drew an all-encompassing circle around what she creates, you would find that the real reason it all works is that she truly loves her students—and they know it.

LIMITLESS LIMITATION

A young child blessed with the gift of autism approached the church pulpit to deliver his prepared speech. He referred regularly to his notes. He spoke with abandon and energy. He was describing all the activities his family had been involved in recently. Then all of a sudden, he looked up, thrust both of his arms straight out toward the congregation, and yelled with explosive excitement, "DISNEYLAND!" What immediately came to my mind was, "that's the way to live; that's the way to love."

For years, I have been pondering the phenomenon of "limitations." I have studied my own and watched others battling through theirs. I have now reached the conclusion from my observations that what the world describes as "limitations" are talents. They are gifts from God who sheds light on how we should view these: "I give men weakness that they may become strong" (Ether 12:27).

The labels of limitation include OCD, ADHD, dyslexia, disorientation, bipolar, borderline personality disorder, autism, overly creative minds, obsessive compulsive, etc. The list is endless. Those who have let these titles, invented by man, limit them are subject to be influenced and even destroyed by the power of suggestion inherent in the titles.

I have watched, on the other hand, people who ignore the titles and BREATHE LIFE into their limitations. When this happens, it is nothing short of beautiful, even miraculous. I have seen autism healed by the saturation of love and constant faith and trust in one's ability to not just reach beyond but "use" the gift of their "weakness" as a sort of springboard or even incentive to create and become. I have seen lists of dyslexics include Einstein, Leonardo Da Vinci, Beethoven, and Handel. I see autistic children mainstreamed, driving, holding jobs, functioning at not only high levels but also highly creative, beautiful levels. I have watched all kinds of psychosis bring to the world genius and creativity beyond possibility.

I have a daughter who was born with 99% right brain creativity. Observing her over the years has convinced me that she has a magic wand hidden inside her somewhere. I call her my Leonardo Da Vinci. She works as a highly esteemed psychological therapist at UCLA. She has been told by the director that she should feel free to do whatever she wants to do because all that she does is so much more creative and ingenious than anything they have ever seen before. This exact thing was told to her in her two previous jobs.

In a movie, Clint Eastwood once said, "A man has got to know his limitations." At first I thought that meant we should accept what we cannot do, and just move on to those we can. I now believe that "knowing" one's limitations can be the most exciting discovery we ever make. We can enjoy them and give credit to them for making us the creative, interesting people we are, and for all that comes to pass because we have decided to "glory" in our weakness, or limitation gifts.

I come from a long heritage of healthy dyslexia and have passed it on to posterity. Our struggle has been some of the most exciting things about our lives. My mother's overly artistic mind and heart "beatings" brought us a prolific array of art in a myriad of forms. A daughter who shares membership with me in a club of genius that the world calls dyslexia writes what only heavenly pens could write. I have been similarly "blessed" and get to jump from one form of artistic expression to the other in an effort to combine all the fireworks going off in my mind.

I have always believed, with all my heart, that to "know" someone is to love them. I believe if we get to "know" our limitations, we will learn to love them. And since "perfect love casteth out all fear," our loving will thrust us out and forward into living a life of faith in our "inabilities," shedding all fear that they need to be hidden in a small, dark room behind a door marked, "LIMITED." We need to love our interesting selves and the interesting people all around us. We are so fascinatingly different and each so marvelously gifted with limitations just waiting for a bellows to blast air into the fire that is waiting to be lit by the rush of air.

KIM

For eight years in Alabama, Kim performed in, produced, and directed musical theatre productions. These productions blessed the community, built the character, and brightened the lives of so many in many beautiful ways.

Before she moved, the community produced an event to honor her for her far-reaching, soul-expansive work, and for the infinite love she had poured out upon the land and into the hearts of all. Everyone who knew her was changed in deep and powerful ways "for good." Everyone wore a T-shirt that night that was created to highlight the philosophy of her heart. The T-shirt read, "Risk! Be Brave. Be Bold. Work Hard. Be Kind. Find the Love. If you're not failing, you're not trying hard enough. Leave your hearts on the stage. Yes! I failed. Yes! I risked. Be 'for' each other. It's always about the other person. I love you. I love you. I love you...Kim Hirt." It is a T-shirt we should all wear— always.

CREATIVE GENIUS

Highly creative minds are gifts from God to this earth. The very special people assigned to house the inspired imagination and creativity of the artistic mind are usually emotionally intense and driven by their need to express what is singing so loudly in their soul. They cannot help but listen to it and then do something about it. W. H. Auden said, "Geniuses are the luckiest of mortals because what they must do is the same as what they most want to do."

Einstein clashed with school authorities and failed an entrance exam. He resented school regimen and restrictive teaching methods and wrote that the spirit of learning and creative thought are lost in strict rote learning.

I watched a child excel beyond possibility in classes that allowed for creative freedom and struggle in classes that allowed for none. Because of what these gifted people end up giving to all of us as they proceed through their lives, I believe we should patiently and reverently allow for the emotional space and freedom of movement needed, so they can respond to the rhythm, the song, and the "beat of a different drum" that plays loudly in their minds and hearts. Because it is so loud, it must be expressed brightly in every art form imaginable.

We then get to sit back on a blanket on the grass and listen, with the expanse of God's creations surrounding us, to Beethoven's Fifth being played at the Boston Commons at the free concert on Friday night...in divine duet.

QUEEN

The Birth of a Queen

On a frosty night in Boston the man I married walked into our family room and said, "We could move to England for a few years, if you would like." My humanities-graduate mind and heart felt like they would explode with happiness at this new possibility. And then we were there—leaving behind the place we had determined we would live and be happy in forever. After living north of London for two years and then moving to California, Washington D.C., Utah, and now Santa Barbara, California, I now, finally, know why.

Katherine the Great—my daughter Katherine the Great—was born there. "Could it be" that she, who has been called "queen of the universe" by her family since she was born, had to be born there?

Did she have to be born on the land where kings and queens have ruled for centuries as a symbol that would breathe up into her soul forever? England has been a place that has called to her ever since and continues to bring her back—as a student and as a traveler—to her "homeland."

Did she need to know that her name was shared by three of King Henry VIII's wives, the French queen, Catherine de' Medici, two empresses of Russia, one of the first Christian saints, Catherine of Alexandria? Did she need to find out later in her life that she was actually a descendant of King Henry VIII and Robert the Bruce?

Did her middle name, Rushforth, a seventh-century English surname that means "river crossing by the rushbeds," help her find the hidden path she would have to take in her life? Did her first name need to mean "pure"? Did her English surname need to mean "champion"?

The Journey of an American Queen

Shakespeare's Polonius said to Laertes, "This above all: to thine own self be true. And it must follow, as the night the day, Thou canst not then be false to any man...my blessing season this in thee!" We all knew, from the very start, that Katherine had the God-ordained responsibility to the world to be "true to her queenly self."

A Day in the Life of the Queen

Four sisters are playing princesses. Katherine is two years old and smaller than most two-year-olds. Her eldest sister informs her that she will be playing the part of princess. She furrows her brow and loudly proclaims across the "land" of our living room: "I'm the Queen!" All the sisters immediately agreed that she, indeed, must be the queen.

This is how it all began and Katherine has remained true to this God-ordained mission: To come to earth and, wherever she is, be the queen. Her parents and nine other siblings can testify, most assuredly, that she has been "true to herself" all her days. We have been taking royal commands from her since she was tiny and have all been blessed by her power wielded across the years of our lives. Her father once said, "I never have any problems with Katherine because I always do what she says."

Among Friends

There was no toleration for bad language, immodesty, or signs of lack of devotion to God. She had the courage to reprimand and encourage in an effort to bring out the best in others.

Going Back

In the sixth grade, Lady (one of her appropriate nicknames) discovered she was not reading at the level of her peers. Not possible—remember, "I'm the Queen!" Through sacrifice, diligence, and a friend who was a godsend, Katherine began to read well. She grabbed hold of her new challenge and put it out in front of her and *commanded* it to serve her. And it obeyed. This forging through, however, was not done without significant collateral damage: self-esteem plummeted.

Another "Could It Be?"

Could it be that Katherine needed to have her queen's place in the world securely in her heart and emblazoned into her soul to make it through what would be a rocky climb through paths of astonishment and discouragement as she forged her way over the next sixteen years?

And then I eventually found myself sitting next to my son—whose academic achievements were accomplished with comparative ease—at Katherine's graduation from college. He looked across at his sister in a huge field of graduates and said, "What Katherine has achieved is monumental and makes anything I have accomplished pale into insignificance." She had received a bachelor of fine arts degree in English. Now she is conquering new territories to be able to teach English and let her story and champion spirit bless the lives of those who will be honored to enter her river crossing through the rushbeds.

Now

Powerful everything. Powerfully influential, powerfully righteous, powerfully bright, spectacularly entertaining, an inspired and inspiring artist, a highly perceptive confidant, deeply loving, endlessly devoted to God, and perfectly true to herself. Whatever there is to do or be in life, she does it with—and is—the essence of magnificence.

It has been our family privilege to watch what can happen when, just "as the night follows the day," a child is true to God, herself, and all mankind.

The Mother's Quest

Our quest is to find out all the "could it be's"—symbolically and in reality—in our children's lives and to look for the miracles and angels and all that continue to announce into our hearts that the hand of God is everywhere. And strive to teach young ones to find the "self" that God is continually opening all our eyes to see.

Could it be the entire reason we moved to Seattle was so Katherine could one day be playing with the daughters of Rojean Garnica, a renowned reading specialist/therapist? Could it be that we moved to England to meet Anita Debney, a revered and trusted friend who is a champion for the betterment of children's lives, who was first to reveal to the world the reality of Katherine's great soul? Could it be?

Katherine—Rushforth—Nelson
Pure—Path Finder—Champion
American Queen

Living happily together builds happily ever after.

CHAPTER TWELVE

Living Happily & Well

PERFECT LIVING IS NOT A REQUIREMENT FOR PERFECT LOVING

We can choose to allow the behaviors that have the potential to be irritants become behaviors of endearment. Each of us has behaviors that may be disturbing to another, since we are all "works in progress."

Let socks on the floor remind us of how hard husbands work for their families each day. Let the clutter and commotion of home and children remind us of the great adventure we all began together when we decided to build our "kingdom on earth" together.

KITCHEN TABLE

Elder LeGrand Curtis said: "One of the most important furnishings found in most homes is the kitchen table."

When I grew up I couldn't wait to gather around the table to hear about all the things my family had done that day. The power of eyes and hearts shooting out back and forth across the table could almost be felt tangibly, creating strong, beautiful, and powerful eternal family bonds.

"I got an A!"

"I made the play!"

"I made the team!"

"I got accepted to college!"

"I ran the mile really fast!"

"I found a snake!"

AGE TRANSCENDENCY

My children were involved in a play together and were celebrating together in a cast party afterwards. I stood back, watched, and realized that everyone was the same age. The people in the cast were of all ages, from very young to very old, but everyone was rejoicing as pure spirits, all differentiations dissolved in the achievement of their unity.

CIRCLE LIVING

God believes in circle living. He asks us to gather together often. He likes us to have family prayer, gather around a table for dinner, and have Family Home Evening all performed in a circle. In a circle, eyes and hearts and spirits connect and reconnect.

NO SPACES

When you enter a classroom, you should make sure there are "no spaces" between people. Everyone should be sitting next to someone. Sitting alone, no matter how emotionally well adjusted you are, makes you feel uncomfortable and lonely. Sitting next to someone warms the spirit.

AUGHT

In a class in church, I heard our teacher teach that if you have "aught" against your brother, you have to go to him and make amends so you can be one like the Savior is one with us and His Father. I raised my hand and asked if it was all right to just overlook and "rise above."

He said, "Absolutely not." He said that subconsciously, we would keep our distance in the future, and be very careful around the person that may have offended us. And that is a "pushing away."

Only those actions that say, "come unto me" are acceptable before the Lord. So if we have "aught," we must do what it takes to fix it, and be one. We should have hearts knit in unity.

NOT IN THE BIBLE

There are so many things that are not "written in the Bible." People can impose so many silly rules on life that restrict you from exploring the wonders of life. Obey every law (the laws of the land; the laws of God), but do not let all those other arbitrary ones inhibit your healthy, safe exploration of this wonderful world.

NOT "FREAKING OUT"

Whenever something would break, spill, or crash, my youngest son and I would practice "not freaking out." We would stop, not move, and examine the situation peacefully. We would talk very calmly, we would take deep breaths, and we would talk about what we were going to do to get through the current trauma. Over time we were able to handle every crisis peacefully, together.

BED

Whenever you clean your room, make the bed first; it gives you hope for the rest of the room.

MORE INCLINED

The exercise you enjoy the most is the one you will be more inclined to do. It doesn't really matter what the exercise is, what matters is how much you like it. And it will change over the years. I ran for twenty years, did aerobics for five years, and did yoga for ten years. The secret is: what you like is what you'll do.

WATER

When you wake up in the morning, your body has just been "decaying" for eight hours. I keep that word in my mind because it helps me remember to drink water when I first wake up and all day long.

One of the habits I have found to help stay "water healthy" is to drink water every time I leave the house and every time I come back home. And I always drink water right before bed to start the cleansing process. Drinking water provides for better general health, weight control, less injury, and greater brightness of mind.

GRANDMA

My grandmother lived with us in England, and while she was there, she became ill for a short period of time. I remember thinking that I should buy flowers and put them in her room because she had to stay there for so many hours every day. I never did it. That was twenty-six years ago.

The other day, I passed some flowers in an open market and thought I should take them to my sister-in-law with whom we were staying while they were still in the process of moving into their home. I was leaving the market and remembered my twenty-six years of regret. I went back and bought the flowers. I hope my Grandma was watching.

RIGHT THING TO DO

My nephew always says, "It was the right thing to do," whenever he has made a good choice or made a sacrifice to participate in something wonderful. This was demonstrated to me one snowy evening when all the cousins and friends were over. Everyone was outside romping in the snow together. It was a perfect, glowing, magical night and I did not go out because I was freezing.

My nephew came in and told me I should have come out—that it would have been "the right thing to do." I have always regretted missing that opportunity and it has taught me to join in on everything; even traveling distances to be present at "right thing to do" events.

The other night we were in a similar situation with everyone wanting to go to the church to play basketball late in the evening. I jumped in with everyone, played terribly, and had a wonderful "right thing to do" with my loved ones.

I will never forget the snowy evening; it keeps me "doing right."

SET THE STAGE

I always think of my home as a stage for life to be played out upon. I believe setting the stage brings a woman great joy—especially as we are able to see how it provides others with an easier and more beautiful way to play out their lives in productive and beautiful ways.

ANNIE'S ROOM

I have decided that my daughter Annie's room is art. It is a painting of all she is and does. You walk in and you see her entire life before you, all at once. It really is beautiful because she lives brightly, beautifully, and full of love for life. Colors of every hue are winding in and out. I love her room; it makes me happy.

CHAIRS ON THE GROUND

When one of my sons was young and frustrated about something in his life, he would go to the kitchen table, from wherever he was in the house, and, one by one grab the back of each of the chairs at the table, and throw the chairs to the ground. He didn't hit, or yell, or express his frustration at anyone. He would just leave and take care of his problem in his "special" way.

One time, an older son ran down to the kitchen, when he knew his brother was about to do this again, and threw all the chairs down before his brother could do it. It made everyone laugh and it became an endearing thing to our family whenever it happened. (Perhaps this highly creative coping mechanism should be submitted to anger management consultants!)

BEST PERSON ON EARTH

Anyone who is doing all they can to be good and do well, without measuring sticks, is the best person on earth.

LISTEN MORE

"Talk A Lot (But Listen More)" is advice I read on the cover of Southwest's Spirit Magazine featuring Mindy Kaling. On a previous trip, I also read advice from a successful businessman who lived by a "let others talk 80%, yourself, 20%" rule. My mind immediately thought of what our greatest example, Jesus Christ, would do if He were to talk with me. I believe these rules would be a given.

SELFISH

I have suffered for years from a disease called "Fear of Missing Out." I would literally writhe, cringe, and suffer deeply from severe emotional, physical, and spiritual pain if I ever missed anything. With a family as large as mine, including children still at home, and children and grandchildren spread across the country—Boston, Washington D.C., Alabama, Oklahoma, San Francisco, Los Angeles, Utah, and Santa Barbara—I was conflicted at every turn as to where to "put myself." I wanted to be everywhere, every second, and miss nothing ever!

Finally, the disease escalated to near madness until an inspired daughter got a hold of me and cured my disease with one word.

She said, "Mom, you are being *selfish!*" (That's the word.) "You are destroying your life, my life, and the lives of everyone around you. Right now, we could be having a wonderful time together by living in our 'now,' but instead you have chosen to whine and carry on about the last thing you had to miss. Also, you are robbing everyone in the house of a creative, new 'now' and you are wasting lots of painful hours on experiences that can never be retrieved from the past, no matter how hard you try."

That was it. I was cured. I have never suffered another minute from that disease. I also find it interesting that this daughter has no recollection of every having said those words to me. I know God was talking through her so I could begin to live a happy, creative life with my family and others. I am grateful for the word, "selfish," for all it has given back to me—"nows" forevermore.

MOVIE STARS

I read an article in a magazine that featured movie stars who were now in their later years. Although their stories varied, there was one thing in common that stood out: They each said that they would trade all the fame, money, the glitz, the glamour—everything—to be able to grow old with someone.

GROW OLD GRACEFULLY

I believe we should grow old gracefully. I believe, however, there are many things that upset the natural flow of growing older. We should, whenever we can, leave our beautiful bodies alone.

I watched my Grandma Bessie grow old gracefully. Right up until the time she passed away, at ninety-three years of age, she was doing yoga, jumping on her mini-trampoline, making her green drinks, and reading every book she could get her hands on—keeping her mind bright and body healthy. She once told me that when you are old, what becomes most important to you is that you are useful. Grandma Bessie was able to use her beautiful, old body to bless the lives of us young'uns until her very last day: nursing relatives through illnesses, helping in the home when granddaughters were bringing new ones into the world, and working tirelessly wherever there was a need. She was gracefully able to make her dreams of being needed come true.

MOVING

Growing up, I moved all over the country: California, Washington, D.C., Arizona, California—and even Venezuela. (One of the moves was three weeks before my senior year.). Since I have been married, we have moved all over the country and to England. We have moved our children irrespective of age or stage or grade, as did my parents.

My great discovery from all these opportunities has been that God is mindful of every person involved in moving from one place to another. It wasn't without tears, but the wealth of experience and expansion of mind that has come from dragging children here, there, and everywhere has been worth all the short-lived heartache.

When I would pick up one of my children from school after that first day in a new place, it seemed as if there was no hope for recovery. I would then wait patiently to hear the words, "I am so glad we moved here!" These words always came with emphasis and gratitude as they watched new opportunities grow into experiences they could not have had in any other way or in any other place: People they would never have met who have become lifelong friends. They have all remarked that it has all, most definitely, "worked for good" in their lives.

My dad, who taught me better than anyone else how to move through life, would often expose us to the wisdom of Dr. Seuss. *Oh, the Places You'll Go!* was, for obvious reasons, a favorite of his in his quest to open the hearts of his seven children to all the possibilities of wonder.

I have written a poem that I dedicate to my father, who was successful in that quest.

LET'S CLIMB OUR TREE

...Don't want to grow up...Please Daddy please
Let me still be the child at your knee
Let me still hear your lullabies sing
Let me still sail upon your wings...

Daughter dear...but can't you see
Come with me...we'll climb our tree
Look out there at mountains high
Look straight up and see the sky
Look at forests...and oceans beyond
And at the soft meadows and lily-filled ponds

You will want to see the world
Watch God's plan for you unfurled
You'll learn to dance and sing and think
Be all grown up before we blink

You'll breathe in all God's hopes for you
And breathe out love in all you do
You'll learn, then teach...you'll save mankind
You'll bless the earth with ties that bind
I've taught you well and you will know
Just what to do and where to go
You'll love the Lord with all your soul
And bring His lost into His fold

And one day Heaven will reach down
And bring new ones...jewels in your crown
And you will bring all life within
Into their hearts...teach where they've been...
And where they'll go...like you and me
You'll climb our tree...show them the sea

And round and round our circles go
Oh, daughter mine...you'll one day know
That searching far and wide will bring
More than any song can sing
You'll love life...its gifts...its days
And seek always His Name to praise...

Signs of Life

It is a beautiful painting of life when you walk in a
home and see backpacks dropped inside the door,

food on the counters, soccer shoes walked out of in the entryway, wet towels in the wrong place, shoes everywhere, and socks definitely everywhere. These are brilliant signs of life: the evidence of lively living at its fullest and brightest; proof that these beautiful people are in your life.

We are often obsessed with putting everything away, apologizing for not having a clean house. A house cluttered with life is still a clean house, but it is better: It is alive!

When my children were small, I would make sure when we did tidy a room, we would set it up for the next round of using and playing with everything. I would tell the older kids that certain toys needed to remain out because we were in the business of family production and part of the processing of life had to do with the little people. It was important they felt that their lives were worthy of physical signs that they were a part of the whole.

Little by little, those signs of life start to leave and you miss those socks. We should treasure each sign. They are all precious.

*Keeping the light of your hopes shining
requires the work of building and tending a fire
all through the night and day after day.*

CHAPTER THIRTEEN

Keeping the Faith

Two "Whens"

When we open our scriptures, we say, "Oh, now I remember who I am and what life is all about."

When we do something wrong, we say, "Oh, I must have forgotten who I am."

Savior's Eyes

If you ever want to know how the Lord feels about you, imagine Him looking into your eyes and you will know.

MOST IMPORTANT WORD

The most important word in the scriptures is the word, *Remember*—that we may always remember Him.

BE THERE

My brother said that he did not know exactly when he gained his testimony of the truthfulness of the gospel, but he attributes it to the fact that our parents made sure we went to everything: every meeting; every fireside; all Young Women, Young Men activities; all ward activities; everything. Over time, all the blessings of obedience combined to build a strong, immovable testimony of the gospel of Christ.

NOT ON MY WATCH

When I was called to teach in the Young Women organization at church, I remember thinking how important it was to make sure none of the Young Women I was in charge of would lose hold of the gospel. To help me remember the importance of my sacred charge over them, I would always say to myself, "Not on my watch."

BIRTH IN A TREE

I once was made aware of an article in a newspaper describing a woman who had to give birth in a tree during a terrible flood. Whenever I am depressed, I think, "At least I am not giving birth in a tree!" It works every time.

STRAIGHT AND CLEAR

My son once said to me, "When you do not have the spirit with you, you do not see clearly and you cannot think straight."

INEXCUSABLE

We run around saying, "That's inexcusable!" No matter how inexcusable it is, it is still forgivable. The Lord made this possible through His infinite atonement.

RIGHTEOUS IN THE DARK

Even when all is pitch black dark and you see no light at all, choose the Lord and the light will come. This is an absolute truth; this is an absolute reality.

Fear is Paralyzing, Faith is Empowering

Fear binds you down and makes your soul crawl into a small, dark cave. The choice to have faith breathes love and life into your soul so you can truly proclaim to the world, "I can do all things through Christ which strengtheneth me."

Peace That Passeth Understanding

The Lord can nurture you with a peace during times of deep and devastating trials that can truly "pass understanding." The depth of His compassion and comfort is not to be understood, only felt. The balm of Gilead embalms the pain.

Under the sea we are taught how this works: a parasite invades the inside of the oyster shell and over time it is nurtured into a glorious, shiny, white pearl.

Devil Laugheth

Imagine what it sounds like to have the Devil laughing at you because he is winning. Do not do anything that will cause him to laugh. You should be the one doing the laughing while saying, "Get thee behind me."

SMARTER THAN GOD

Whenever I am tempted to do something that I know would not meet God's approval, I stop and say to myself, "Oh, you must think you are smarter than God." I know the laws of God, the word of God, and the counsel from prophets are all to help me live the "plan of happiness." I try to never live "smarter than God."

GET ON A MOTORCYCLE

If you are ever in a situation where you are beginning to feel desperate and are losing perspective on life (you feel like life is not worth living anymore), get on a motorcycle and feel the wind in your hair and on your face. Ride up into the mountains and look out over the world.

You will realize that no matter what is happening in life, the world will keep on turning. And if you hang on and just keep going, things will eventually turn out right. Just keep going. And whether you fail your final exam in Math or not is not really all that important in the grand scheme of things. Take the class again next semester—or not.

KNOW NOT WHAT THEY DO

Think of the times we disappoint ourselves: we think we are going along in the right direction, but somehow because of our weaknesses everything turns upside down. Sometimes our best ends up being not quite good enough, and that is when the Lord says, "Forgive them, for they know not what they do."

If you think about it, even when we do really wrong things, we "know not what we do," because if we were completely aware, completely in tune with the Spirit, completely aware at that very moment that we are of royal heritage as sons and daughters of God himself, we would not have done wrong. But because of where we might be in life—sometimes dark, sometimes lost—we make our offering, however great or pathetic, and the Lord looks up to God for us and says, "Forgive them, for they know not what they do." It is a plea to Heavenly Father to be patient with our struggling souls as we try to work it all out here on earth.

ROBOT

When I was young, I made a promise to God that I would read the scriptures every day and never, ever miss a day, no matter where I was or how hard it would be to do this. As I was wandering through the maze of life, I found myself thrust into a very dark time that made me unable to see the light for a long while. I would open my eyes and see black.

Still, I was used to reading the scriptures everyday, robotically. The habit was so deeply programmed into my behavior that God could still reach me because I would read His words, almost unaware that I was.

After a long process with His voice singing into my soul, my life was saved. My early commitment to God allowed me to hear Him "through the black." I don't believe He could have reached me any other way, but He did, and the words that "glowed" into my heart eventually healed me as only the Master could.

No Rules

When you are processing grief beyond what is possible to bear it is important to have "No Rules." You can read all the books and hear all the counsel you care to let in, but as you and the Lord work together with all your might to heal your broken heart, there should be no rules for how fast you process or how you process. It is a personal partnership.

Loved ones who care can help, but ultimately you set the pace. You set the rules—no rules. Let yourself feel the slow or fast balm of Gilead. Let it happen how it will, but always know it will.

CHURCH MEETINGS
I am so glad I was there today. Imagine what I would have missed learning, feeling, committing, and strengthening.

LOT'S WIFE
When I anguish over missed opportunities for my loved ones and myself, I choose to think of Lot's wife who looked back longingly instead of facing forward and turned into a pillar of salt. Faith has everything to do with the future and nothing to do with the past.

IN THE FIGHT
Sometimes we believe that we are bothering or disappointing our Father in heaven while we are processing our messy lives. We aren't if we are still "in the fight" and haven't given up. He loves us. He can "take" a lot, just like we can. He is proud of us for staying in the ring.

SEMINARY STUDENT

If you want to catch a glimpse of the best people on the earth, peek into a window of a class of early-morning seminary students: high school students who choose to learn about God and His word at six o'clock in the morning. There just are no better people.

TRUE

"Some things are true whether you believe them or not." (This is a quote from a movie starring Nicolas Cage.) God has provided, within us, all we need to discover and know what is true.

MOON

Etched in the heart of the moon are the many moments my children and I have stood at a bedroom window before going to sleep and said, "moon, moon!"

And as they grew older: "The moon is shining!" which opened their hearts to speak of all the wonderful things that were important at that time in their young lives. Decades of children's hearts have now passed through my heart and I still, before going to bed, look up and proclaim, "The moon is shining on us tonight!"

Recently, after a yearlong trial with no apparent end in sight, I looked up at the moon and said, "The moon is not shining on us anymore." I then closed the blinds and went to sleep. The very next day the year of "faith's struggle to rise above fear" ended. I think the Lord did not want me thinking the moon was not shining on us—even for one night. I will never close my blinds again.

"Taught from on high" is our chance to "hold hands with God" in bringing His light into His World.

CHAPTER FOURTEEN

Words to Live By

THERE IS NO TRY

In the movie *Star Wars*, Yoda said, "Try not. Do or do not. There is no try."

Trying usually means not doing. Failure is built into the word already.

JUST TWO

Just two things: one is a number and one is a letter. In our church, we are counseled not to date until we are *sixteen*, and we are told to not attend *R*-rated movies. These things are so definitive and clear that they should be easy to follow.

SIDEWAYS LIVING

Avoid "sideways living" whenever possible. So much of our time is spent side by side: riding in a car; sitting in front of the television; talking as we walk next to each other; sitting at a movie, play, ballgame, etc. What is missing are the eyes. The window to the soul is left out and there is no real exchange of heart, spirit, and soul.

Whenever I go on a date with my husband, I make sure that at some point we are sitting across from each other so we can see each other for who we really are. "Oh! There you are!"

THE ETERNAL ORDER

1. God
2. Spouse
3. Children
4. Extended Family
5. Others

Things go beautifully when life is lived in "order." We are often conflicted about how to use our time and about which endeavors or causes we should involve ourselves. It becomes much easier with this as an eternal guideline for everyday living.

As a grandmother with a child still at home, I have found it to be very important to not lose my footing as I spread myself out among all those who might need me (family, church, community, etc.). God can help us each see clearly how to use the talent and time he had given us so "we can all edify one another together."

YOU ARE WHAT YOU DO
In the end, it is not what you say—but what you do that matters. You can speak with power and conviction, but until you live with power and conviction, it is all for naught.

BE IN THE MOMENT
Live right where you are, right in the moment, or you will miss *everything*!

EVERY DAY 'TIL THE DAY YOU DIE
My Grandma Bessie, who lived to age ninety-three, said that we should exercise our bodies "everyday 'til the day you die."

She was still doing yoga in her nineties. She lived out her final years taking care of people twenty, thirty, and forty years younger than herself.

START

I asked a daughter to tell me what she would give as advice to solve the problem of procrastination. She said, "Start!" Starting is the hardest part.

She said that if you just put the idea in your mind right at the beginning, then it lives in your mind subconsciously, and without you knowing it, pulls you toward your goal of finishing whatever you are working on. Starting is the secret.

COME UNTO ME

Any action or thought that, in essence, does not say, "come unto me," as the Lord says, will bring unhappiness to you and the receiver. All will lose. If you open your arms and heart and live with "come unto me" in your soul, your life will be full, abundant, and joyful.

OUT OF THIS WORLD

Taking yourself out of this world is "out of this world." There is so much more joy in feeding your soul with what the Lord has to offer than with what the world has to offer. Be good to yourself by choosing good things.

No Black Holes

When you are taking pictures of people, do not let them wear their sunglasses. You cannot see their eyes and it looks like everyone just has black holes for eyes.

The eyes are the windows to the soul—don't let them cover their eyes.

And when you talk to people, take off your sunglasses so they can see your eyes and you can see theirs. Otherwise it is like talking to black holes—no soul.

Too Many Voices

Sometimes it is time to close all the books and turn off all the voices. Too many opinions can cloud what God is telling you in your heart. Let Him speak, and then you can gather information and set it aside. Let yourself be "taught from on high."

Tragedy

There is no tragedy in death—only in sin. Losing a loved one to death breaks our heart only for the time of mortality. Losing a loved one to sin and transgression breaks our heart for an eternity.

CRINGES

Cringes are good things. They are signs that you have been in the fight and swarm of life. They are signals that you are giving it your all.

Cringes come with the territory of living. Doing things that later make you shudder means you are in the game of life, and playing with all your heart and soul.

A life of shuddering is better than closing yourself in your house and never talking to anyone or doing anything.

TWENTY-FIVE MILES PER HOUR

I was complaining to my adult son about getting a speeding ticket for only driving eight miles over the speed limit in a twenty-five mile an hour zone.

I was expecting to hear him say, "Oh man, that's ridiculous. I can't believe they would do that—that is just not fair!"

Instead he said, "What if by going the speed limit at that time you were able to save a child's life?"

I will never forget that. It has reminded me that "limits" are what keep us safe on every level of life. They are sacred gifts.

LIGHT THE FIRE

We all have things that we can choose to hang on to in our past. We hang on to them by "lighting a fire" underneath them. Every day we have a choice: light it or stamp it out. I think this is one of the uses of "firmness of mind."

WHAT YOU CARE ABOUT

God always cares about what you care about. If it is important to you, it is important to Him. Let Him know.

ANGELS

In the scriptures, the first words angels say are, "Fear not." We should live lives of faith and fullness, not fear.

MONEY OR THE MIRACLES

My sister-in-law, Marlena, has become famous in our family for this motto she has always lived by: God can cause so many more "wonders to behold" and miracles upon miracles than any money could ever buy.

THERE'S ALWAYS A STORY

Whenever you are quick to make a judgment about what someone is doing that you cannot figure out, remember "there is always a story." When you stop and find out what caused someone to do what they did, compassion replaces judgment and anger.

I heard a story told by a religious leader in our church that caused him to ponder the reality of this idea. He was in his car and accidentally tapped the backend of someone's car. He was surprised when the man got out of his car and unleashed every foul word imaginable upon him. The next Sunday, he was also surprised to see this man in the congregation where he was about to give a talk.

After the meeting, the man he tapped came up to apologize for his outrageous behavior, and then continued to explain that at the time his car was bumped, he was just in the middle of trying to figure out how to tell his children, when he got home, that their mother had just died. When his car was bumped, it was the last straw for him, and therefore, the unleashing. When the "story" was revealed behind the man's actions, understanding and compassion replaced all the initial surprise.

"There is always, always a story." Take time to listen to it, first. God told us to leave all judgment to Him. When I think about why He asked us to do this, I think of all the stories behind why I do things, why my children do things, why all people do things, and even if we try to figure out their stories, we really don't know anyone's "real" story. God alone knows our true history.

Letting go of judging from our limited perspective is so liberating. And realizing that we are all in the hands of God, thankfully, allows us to let go and love—just love—without judgment. The stories of people's lives can then be written more beautifully, with our love supporting them, without interference.

HEART TRUTH

"Buy my idea!"

I have discovered there are two kinds of truth: truth that rings true to the heart, mind, and soul together, and truth that is being sold to whoever does not take the time to think about it. One of the most significant times in my life that woke me up and taught be to be careful of all the "voices" shouting into my mind was when I began to raise my first child. I read books full of new ideas and listened to the advice of others. What I discovered was that some of the old ideas that have "rung true to the heart" for ages were being sacrificed at great "cost." Since old ideas don't sell anymore, people are coming up with new ideas that sometimes don't make sense at all and are completely out of harmony with what we know to be true in our hearts. God gave every man that is on the earth the means to know for himself what is true. It takes a quiet minute to figure it out, but it can be done, and it needs to be done.

I once read a magazine article written by a man who had many impressive degrees accompanying his name. He presented his beautifully written argument that "miracles have ceased on the earth." When I read that, I knew it was untrue. I knew it immediately because I, like everyone else in the world, have a spirit of discernment within me. My own life, which is filled with endless miracles every single day, spoke much louder to me than the evidence presented by this scholar of theology. The age of information is a marvelous age to live in. If we are careful, we can participate in the great enlightenments that are available. If we are going to "buy" into it, however, let us be wary of "money truth" and spend our time and money on gathering "heart truth."

Ponderous thoughts grow powerful thoughts and powerful lives.

CHAPTER FIFTEEN

Thoughts to Ponder

BODY WILL REQUIRE

You can spend all your days sick and moaning in bed or you can exercise, eat well, and be actively engaged in a good cause. They both require the same amount of time. The body requires a decision about how you will treat it, but the demand of time is the same.

THE ONLY PROBLEMS YOU HAVE

My sister said, "The only problems you have are the lessons you have not learned."

The same old problems just keep reoccurring until we make a change or have a "mighty change of heart."

CRYING IN THE NIGHT

When someone says, "just kidding," after saying something derogatory, there is usually "crying in the night." One may act like it did not affect him or her, but it always does. Anything you say that is followed by just kidding should never be said.

ONE MEASLY LIFETIME

A dear friend of mine was talking to me about her daughter and wondering when she was going to choose happiness for herself. She then said, "We should be able to pull off one measly lifetime."

LAMP BY THE BEDSIDE

You cannot live without a lamp by your bedside. When you read scriptures at night under your covers, and know that in a minute you have to get out of bed to turn off the light, you end up just turning out the light on your way in and jumping into bed—no scriptures.

With a lamp by the bedside, you read and then just reach over and turn out the light. There is no way to live without the light of the scriptures pouring into your soul.

AMERICAN

There are so many blessings and freedoms that come with being an American citizen in this great country. When I think of this, I feel so blessed that it wipes out any kind of "off" feeling I may temporarily be feeling that day.

WHERE IS THE PARTY?

My friend said that she was always too nervous to have people over because she felt her house had to be absolutely perfect before she would ever feel comfortable.

She went to a big party where everyone was having the time of their lives, and really, truly enjoying one another. She looked at the kitchen floor that was not very clean and saw that not everything was in perfect order. She then thought, "Where is the party?" No one ever came to her perfectly, clean house, but there they all were, dirty floor and all. Have parties anyway.

START WITH "NO"

We will be told many times in our lives that something is not possible. If someone says no, begin there. If your cause is just, go to the top for help. The person who is being paid $3.00 an hour is not going to help you and why should they? The people who have a vested interest in their company or program will help you because they care about being successful and making people happy with what they are providing. Writing letters to presidents of companies and corporations should be the next step to any initial answer of "no."

A good part of my parents' house burned down and the insurance company offered a very small amount of money to compensate for the damages. My parents were about to accept this until they thought more about it and decided it was preposterous. They went back to the company and explained the situation, and they were awarded a much, much larger sum of money. "No" is where you begin, not where you end.

SPORTS

I heard men talking about sports on the radio. They said that women should learn that they must never, ever say, "It is only a game." The announcers went on to say that, to men, sports is life!

ONCE WE WERE HERE

In the final scene of the movie *Last of the Mohicans*, the Mohican father looks out over the vast cavern and talks about all the people that will soon come in and struggle and fight to create a new life. Then he says, "but once we were here...."

Sometimes my husband and I would stand in front of our beautiful Highland, Utah, home and look out at the mountains behind us. We would look at all the homes and winding paths that house and connect all the people we love and it was overwhelming to us. All the beauty. All the love. And as we pondered our upcoming move to Santa Barbara, we'd say, "but once we were here." And we planned to keep it all in our hearts forever and ever.

BROADCAST
Millions of dollars are spent on live church broadcasts. If "Oh, well, it doesn't matter, I can just read it in the church bulletin or online later," were just as good, why would the church "waste" so much money? There is a reason—a powerful reason.

YELL AND HEAL
God doesn't care if we yell at Him. Sometimes it is just how we, as God's children, feel. The reason He doesn't care is because we are still looking up at Him. As long as we keep our eyes on Him, we will eventually stop yelling and start healing. The secret

is never to take your eyes off of Him and "all will be well" in the end. He is the Master Healer.

TEMPLE—OCEAN

I believe if it were impossible to build temples on the earth, the Lord would have us "attend" the ocean regularly. The beauty, light, life, and symbolism that are everywhere brighten and bless and clear the mind.

TOUCH IT ONCE

When dealing with clothes, remember to touch them only once—hang them up immediately—or else you will have to waste energy by touching them twice.

JUST GOING TO KOHLERS

When saying goodbye is just too hard to do, just say, "We'll see you at Kohler's" (the corner grocery store).

GAMES

It has been proven that when men play competitive games, their stress level goes down, and for women it goes up. Conversely, when women play noncompetitive games, their stress level goes down, and for men it goes up.

LIFE À LA "I"/"EYE"

I have lots of favorite things. If I were the *Sound of Music*'s Maria, jumping on the bed with the seven Von Trapp children and singing, "These Are a Few of My Favorite Things," the list would go on and on. One of those very, very favorite things would be looking into the faces of my children. There have been times, I have to admit, when my children have looked at me, and whatever I was about to say to them just went away—the lecture, the admonition, the counsel—just melted away into complete adoration as I beheld their freckled, dimpled, green/blue eyed, smiling faces.

This favorite thing, however, is something I find much more difficult to find now. The tops of my children's heads are now becoming more familiar to me. Technology has transformed my accessibility to those shining "eyes" to "i's"...iPad, iPhone, and iPod.

My brother, who is a doctor at Stanford University, commented that there is a new general posture among the students there as they walk across campus: bent over and staring at their iPhones.

I go to church and people all around me are holding iPads. We used to be able to cozy-up to one another, share a hymnal, and join our voices together to sing praises. Now, we sit next to hard, flat, heavy iPads. And while our "eyes" used to be fixed upon the speaker who worked so hard to provide us with an inspired message, we now peruse the scriptures or the planets or other gospel related topics or check e-mail. Eyes are down, and iPads are open. Little children can't help but be distracted by the wealth of possibilities for distraction in the magical iPad—the new-age "quiet book."

We all walk around "hooked up," or rather "hooked down," unable to "see" all that is around us that continually testifies, in beautiful ways, that God is all around us, especially in the eyes of all the people in our lives, which is the ultimate gift of life.

I believe the greatest "scientific" discovery that Leonardo Da Vinci made is that the eye is "the window of the soul."

I wonder if we participated in a worldwide experiment together, could we get our "eyes" back? What if we left our iPhones and iPads in the car whenever we entered a restaurant, or a church, or a movie, or anywhere we might have the chance to look into the "windows of the soul" of the person who at that moment in time is our gift from God? These moments are often lost to whoever happens to be on the phone at the time, who is apparently more important than the person standing in front of us. We could discover that the grocery clerk just returned from Hawaii where he celebrated his twentieth wedding anniversary, or that the teenager working behind the McDonald's cash register is about to compete in a state tennis tournament.

Relieved of our devices, we, along with the students at Stanford University, could stand up straight again and behold the wonders of the earth—the expansive wonders of God's gifts—and enjoy, once again, the greatest wonder of all—each other, eye to eye.

HISTORY ALIVE

As I walk the streets of Charleston, South Carolina, and Savannah, Georgia, with my girls—I can feel it, it is everywhere: the vitality of all those who have played their part on the grand stage of life. It is recorded beneath your feet, in the wind, in the

Spanish Moss hanging from the trees, in pictures and paintings of faces and families who stare back at you with life's light in their eyes, in the white sand, in the swamps, in the homes that were burned down over and over again by war and mishap, in the graveyards with tiny tombstones of those who lived hours or days, or ninety-five years, down plantation lanes, and along the rivers. You hear it in the clomping horses, and the sad and happy stories being whispered and shouted and sung of emancipation. You see it in the tears and smiles, in the big and bright cooking, and in the pride and glory. I have never felt "dead and gone" feel so alive.

TREASURES

When I was a young girl, my Grandma Bessie told me a story about a dear neighbor friend who passed away. After several years her husband remarried. As they became acquainted with their new neighbor, Grandma Bessie and her friends noticed that all the treasures, heirloom linens, and valuables that their friend had stowed away for years—too valuable to use or display—were all being used on a daily basis and displayed everywhere in the home. As they watched the new wife enjoy all the things they knew their friend never allowed herself to enjoy while she was alive, they determined that this was not going to happen to them!

So out came everything. They started using all their fine china and linens. Once-hidden keepsakes were now placed where they could see them. It no longer mattered that they might break or get worn out. All around them now were beautiful things that gladdened their hearts and filled their minds with sweet memories.

You can probably imagine, as the mother of ten children, that I have seen amazing amounts of broken, crashed, and destroyed—and because of the lesson learned at my grandmother's knee, I have probably provided opportunity for more things to break than a seemingly wiser approach would have allowed.

The other day I was reminded of my long-held determination to be true to my grandma. I have a smiling sunshine plate that was painted by my seven-year-old daughter, Annie, twelve years ago. It makes me happy everyday. I noticed a few days ago that it had been broken and then carefully glued back together. It was not perfect anymore, but the sunshine of my Annie was still smiling back at me. The beautiful thing about this is that I haven't missed a day of Annie's sun shining into my heart for twelve years.

Things I Would Want My Children to Know

I would want to tell my children:

- How grateful I am to have them in my life and for the blessing of being able to love them
- That they are more deeply a part of my soul and all that I am than they could ever imagine
- That I yearn and pray and beg constantly for the power of heaven, the love of heaven, to pour down upon their heads so that all their dreams may come true

- That their righteousness is my only treasure on this earth
- That their efforts to bind themselves to Christ and His cause and His precious gospel is all the hope of my heart
- That the name of Jesus Christ will stay brightly emblazoned upon their souls and be worn humbly and proudly and bravely as a banner of who they are—children of Christ
- That to the degree they live the gospel of Christ is the degree to which they will be happy, and their happiness is all my happiness
- That the heritage of their great grandparents should be honored by always "being there"—being everywhere—so as to serve and reap in the cause of Christ
- That any love held back will be their only pain

I want my children to:
- Marry the heart
- Live in circles that connect your souls and eyes
- Keep a lamp and the scriptures by your bedside

- Let the word of God save your life
- Stay so clean and pure that you can be like Nephi where anything you ask will be granted to you because of your exceeding righteousness and purity
- Let the "wind" of the atonement take it all away and do not chase it
- Look up
- Let all your actions speak "Come unto Me"
- Hold on tight to one another so we can all "Be There" in heaven with no one missing

I want to thank:
- Darci for teaching me how to really see the ocean and for being our "Guardian of the Galaxy"
- Jimmie for teaching me to see others through God's eyes and for being our "Child Whisperer"
- Christie for the magical power of her love and creativity
- Kimberley for her spirit of inhibition and her angel faith
- Katherine for her undaunted nobility and champion spirit
- Sam for showing me what the radiance of the sun feels like when it is within someone

- Fred for showing me what clean, white purity looks like in someone's eyes
- Annie for her loving heart and being willing to share her endless talents
- Tom for his love for spiritual things and for letting me play the part of Aragorn when we played Lord of the Rings in the woods
- Jack for letting me enjoy and spoil him and for being the person that all his brothers and sisters say is the greatest thing I have ever done in my life
- And my husband who works hard so I can stay home to be a mother to our children; he who lives every moment of his life trying to make all our dreams come true; he doesn't know that he doesn't need to work so hard at it because all my dreams came true the day I found him on this earth; no words have been fashioned yet to describe my gratitude and love for him—so those words I am unable to speak yet...maybe in heaven

About the Author

KAREN MANN NELSON's passion for writing began when she was a young girl, which created a clear path for her education. She received her BA in Humanities at Brigham Young University. She is the mother of ten children, which opened up endless possibilities for her writing.

Her philosophies for life were largely driven by wanting to write down all the "at your knee" teachings that exploded from her desire to leave her children with solid, "things I would want my children to know."

She also involved her children in the performance and production of "Life of Christ" community concerts for nearly twenty years and this added another dimension of soul-expansion in her quest to open her children's minds to the idea of endless possibility.

Karen served as California Mother of the Year in 2011, which was her chance to teach powerful, reasonable, "listen to your own heart and to what makes sense to your mind" motherhood. She has also worked extensively in the Women's and Young Women's Organization in her church, which has created another avenue for her to teach her vision for how to live "without the voices."

Karen is currently involved in a charity to emotionally and spiritually rescue women and children of the world.

Karen and her husband of forty-two years have raised their children all over the world and currently reside in Santa Barbara, California.

Karen's primary blog is at
www.KarenVedaNelson.com

Follow Karen Nelson via
Twitter:
https://twitter.com/karenmannnelso1

Facebook:
https://www.facebook.com/karen.v.nelson.9

Made in the USA
San Bernardino, CA
17 April 2017